This Is My Story

Candi Staton

This Is My Story

Printed in the United States of America

This Is My Story
ISBN 1-56229-422-9

Pneuma Life Publishing
4451 Parliament Place
Lanham, MD 20706
(301) 577-4052
www.pneumalife.com

Contents

Dedication
Acknowledgments
Foreword
Introduction
Discography

Chapter   Page

Dedication

This book is dedicated first to Jesus Christ, who is the Lord of my life and the Author and Finisher of my faith.

To my husband, Pastor John Sussewell.

To my children: Marcel Williams, Marcus Williams, Terrence Williams, Cassandra Hightower and Clarence Carter, Jr.

To all my beautiful grandchildren: Derek, Angel Elaine, Jasmine, Jeneka, Brandon, Brionca, Nikki, Canzetta, Cameron, Destiny Joya, Callen, Landon, Christina, Timothy, Cannady, and Tamika.

To my one son-in-law, Calvin Hightower, and my four daughters-in-law: Mona Williams, Jenny Williams, Costina Williams, and Tasha Carter.

Acknowledgments

To Frank Edmonson (aka 'Paul Baker') who took this work from my own handwriting (which was a miracle to interpret) and put it into the first draft. Thanks for helping me to realize this vision. God bless you.

To Barbara Anderson; thank you for helping me to complete some chapters during the second draft. I love you.

To Debbie Bartlett who encouraged me to write this book. When I thought I only had a testimony, you said, "Girl, this is a book. Finish it and put it out." You sowed the first monies to make it possible. Thank you Debbie for believing in me.

Dianna Cherry and Tony Foxx for helping me edit this work. You are a blessing. I will forever be grateful to you. Love you both.

Foreword

It is a great joy and a special privilege to write the foreword of, This Is My Story, the touching autobiography of Candi Staton.

I have always appreciated Candi's relationship with God, her reverential awe of His holiness, and her unyielding faith in His omnipotence. Candi's unwavering trust in God through difficult trials, tests, and temptations has been an inspiration to me. It is a blessing to see a minister who lives the Gospel that she sings and preaches.

This Is My Story gives us a look into Candi Staton's past – its ups, downs, challenges, and bright moments. It tells the story of her rise from a blighted background to fame, fortune, and the bright lights. This story reveals the importance of sowing seeds of God's Word into the hearts of our children at an early age. Although Candi turned to the world's "big time," those seeds sown in her heart as a young girl provided a contact point for her in times of desperation, to hear from God and to be touched by Him.

This Is My Story gives hope to those who feel their situation is hopeless. Remember, there are no hopeless people, just people who feel helpless in seemingly hopeless situations. Anyone, especially a female, who has ever gone through a trial, test or temptation will be touched with the experiences that Candi shares in This Is My Story.

The God of Candi Staton is the God who works in our hopelessness. As you read this book, may you be encouraged, inspired, and most of all, changed by God.

Mrs. (Dr.) Dianna Cherry
Full Gospel A.M.E. Zion Church
Temple Hills, Maryland

Introduction

CANDI STATON's involvement with American music has brought her recognition not only in the United States, but in numerous countries around the world. Her unique singing style and voice has gained the respect and admiration not only of fans, but also of fellow vocalists and musicians.

Candi's public performing has gone full circle: from church singing, through concert/club performances of pop, rhythm & blues, record contracts, gold records (both domestic & internationally), and on to even greater dimensions afforded by her rich talent, most recently including song writing. Along the way she has gained the experience and maturity to firmly direct her career exactly where she wants it. Now, as a psalmist in ministry, she has gained the sensitivity and discernment to recognize that such focus and resolve is through the direction and anointing of the Holy Spirit.

Candi has recorded seventeen albums during her colorful career: three for CAPITOL RECORDS, two for UNITED ARTISTS, six for WARNER BROTHERS, one for SUGAR HILL, and six on BERACAH RECORDS.

Public appearances as a solo artist were with such notables as Eddy Arnold, Roy Clark, John Davidson, Alex Drier, Marty Robbins, and Sammi Smith. She also shared the stage in the same capacity with Mac Davis, Lou Rawls, Al Green, Bobby Womack, Freda Payne, Ashford & Simpson, Diana Ross, Stephanie Mills, Teddy Pendergrass, Aretha Franklin, B.B. King, Boz Scaggs, Little Richard, The Commodores, Johnny Mathis, and Donny Hathaway.

Each year brought Candi more recordings and more concerts. There were yet more cherished accolades that would honor her unique artistry and influence as a "stylist." In 1971, she was nominated on the final ballot for her first GRAMMY AWARD with "Stand By Your Man." In the next year, she headlined her own sellout performance at the Flamingo Ballroom in Las Vegas. In 1973, she appeared on 21st Century Productions' "SOUND AMERICA", which aired on CBS Television, and received her second GRAMMY nomination for the recording of "In The Ghetto." In 1975, she was the special guest of Dick Clark on AMERICAN BANDSTAND. In 1977, she opened for Ray Charles at the Alladin Theater in Las Vegas. In 1978, she co-starred with Lou Rawls on NBC- TV's MIDNIGHT SPECIAL, and a year later she was an invited guest of President Jimmy Carter during the Black Music Association Dinner on the White House lawn, accompanied by such luminaries as Andre Crouch, Joe Williams, and Chuck Berry.

While she continued recording blockbuster hits, such as "Young Hearts Run Free" and "Victim", both million sellers, she entertained audiences around the globe. Countries she visited included Peru, Venezuela, Australia, South Africa, France, Germany, Holland, the Caribbean Islands, Nigeria, Sweden, the United Kingdom, and other parts of Europe, South America, and Africa.

In all the years of her singing, she had never written songs entirely by herself. It was in 1982 that Candi, following a dramatic turn in her life, began creating a flow of dynamic compositions which has continued to the present. These songs are a vivid testimony to the "new direction" in which Candi is now headed.

Candi's first release, "MAKE ME AN INSTRUMENT", broke into the #7 mark (for sales) on the BILLBOARD SPIRITUAL chart shortly after its release, and subsequently garnered her third GRAMMY AWARD nomination. Candi's fourth GRAMMY nomination came in 1987 with "Sing A Song", a widely advertised release opening up ministry opportunities in several countries abroad including Japan, Korea, Philippines, Australia, Kenya, Uganda, South Africa, England, Sweden, Canada, etc.

In 1989 Candi was honored with a nomination for the DOVE AWARD under the auspices of the GOSPEL MUSIC ASSOCIATION for her performance on the "Love Lifted Me" album. Now in 1992, the GMA has voted Candi again to be among those few final ballot nominees for the DOVE with the title "STANDING ON THE PROMISES."

In response to the popularity of all of Candi's albums and the refreshing, inspiring and Spirit filled content of Candi's songs, she appears frequently on Christian television stations and their "flagship" programs. In addition, Candi has completed an eight year run of her own television series entitled "NEW DIRECTION," carried weekly on the TRINITY BROADCASTING NETWORK.

Candi's current weekly music format on TBN is dubbed "SAY YES..." an upbeat yet uncompromised message targeted to embattled individuals and families in the nation's urban communities.

Such exposure makes CANDI STATON the most widely televised gospel singer/psalmist from among those who have had a former "mainstream," secular music career on major labels.

Local communities and church fellowships across America and abroad, have benefited greatly from Candi's ministry, as she sings, preaches and testifies before their gatherings. In a generation where so many popular music performers have abandoned their gospel roots in order to seek fame and fortune, Candi is one of only two (2) former major secular artists to uncompromisingly return to those roots with a conviction, sincerity and consistency that is truly exemplary! Such commitment, coupled with the anointing of the Holy Spirit, results in Candi being requested to minister along side of many of today's most respected leaders in the five-fold ministry.

Yet there is another aspect of Candi's ministry which has been elusive for gospel artists. As a Christian who happens to be Afro-American, Candi's appeal is strong among audiences in her own community. Yet her songs are 'Gospel' in every sense of the Word (as compared to the 'positive pop' being pawned off as gospel today by the music industry). Candi's stylistic artistry has succeeded in bringing down ethnic barriers, resulting in a much wider audience acceptance than her peers by those mature in the Faith.

Candi's resolve to stick to the gospel in her music is infectious. There is an assurance and security in her life that passes through her and into the hearts and minds of those hearing her. She reminds her audiences that a person can stand firm and stand tall in life. She also reminds them that they have to weaken their own pride enough to acknowledge the Son of the Living God, Christ Jesus, whose Spirit and grace alone is sufficient to enable and empower them. Anything less, she declares, is compromise — and compromise is not a word in CANDI STATON's conversation.

There are doubtless hundreds of thousands of CANDI STATON 'fans' — those from the past and present — and some sure to be made in the future — who will be inspired by her faith. So much so that their own lives will be changed to the glory of God The Father and His Son, Jesus Christ!

Candi Staton Discography

"I'd Rather Be An Old Man's Sweetheart..."		Fame, '69
"I'm Just A Prisoner"		Capitol, '70
"Sweet Feeling"		Capitol, '70
"Stand By Your Man"	Grammy Nominated	Capitol, '71
"He Called Me Baby"		Capitol, '71
"In The Ghetto"	Grammy Nominated	United Artists, '73
"Do It In The Name Of Love"		United Artists, '74
"Music Speaks Louder Than Words"		Warner Bros., '75
"Young Hearts Run Free"		Warner Bros., '77
"Victim"		Warner Bros., '78
"Chance"		Warner Bros., '79
"Looking For Love"		Warner Bros., '80
"Nitelites"		Sugar Hill, '81
"Make Me An Instrument"	Grammy Nominated	Beracah, '83
"The Anointing"		Beracah, '85
"Sing A Song"	Grammy Nominated Stellar Nominated	Beracah, '86
"Love Lifted Me"	Dove Nominated	Beracah, '88
"Stand Up & Be A Witness..."		Beracah, '89
"Standing On The Promises"	Dove Nominated	Beracah, '91
"I Give You Praise"		Beracah ,'93

Chapter 1

Dreamer Of A Dream

I was born in Hanceville, Alabama, in a little community called "The Colony." It was totally populated by blacks. Some of the men who lived there worked in a nearby coal mine, but most of the families made their living by farming.

I can still hear the sounds of the plowers and farmers yelling at the mules. "Gee!" and "Hah!" meant right and left to them. Sometimes, I would wake up at 4:30 in the morning and follow my father to the fields, to walk behind him as he turned the earth, preparing to plant the crop. I'll never forget the smell or feel of that fresh-turned earth, it was so refreshing to my bare feet.

When I was 5 years old I discovered I could sing. We had invited the members of a Pentecostal church to visit our Baptist church. One little girl that they brought along could really sing and when I heard her that Sunday, I wanted to sing more than anything. I began to pray and ask God to let me sing, too. I remember that I would often try to sing, but my young voice wouldn't hold a tune! I got frustrated learning, but I kept on trying!

One day another group of Pentecostals came through our small community seeking a place to start a revival. They went to our church first but the pastor said no. They went to every church in the neighborhood and got the same answer.

The Pentecostals then went to several homes, but everyone said, "Oh no!" because they were afraid of them. They had heard a rumor that these Pentecostals would throw strange dust on you that would cause you to lose your mind. No one wanted to be near them.

They came to our house, and my mother opened our doors to them. We moved all of the furniture out of our small living room and they set up their drum set.

They started to sing and play. I had never heard such a joyful noise in my life! They were beating the drums, shaking their tambourines, clapping their hands, singing, dancing, and talking funny talk. A few of our neighbors began to gather on the outside and a few wandered in, but no one wanted to get too close. I was so small that I didn't understand it all but I knew one thing — I liked the beat.

When the revival was over and the "saints" left, everything was almost back to normal, except for my sister and me. Those people had made quite an impact on us. We found two buckets and a wash tub and a few sticks of wood, and the beat went on day after day.

"Calm down, you two!" our mama would shout at us. We'd move further from the house and start up again.

I was especially excited the day I discovered I had learned one of the songs those Pentecostals had sung and could sing it myself. I could sing! I got better and better and soon learned to do tricks with my voice, creating my own runs and my own style of singing.

One day as I was beating my bucket drum in the back of the house, one of my mother's friends was eavesdropping and found out I could sing. So, the next Sunday, when our pastor came from Birmingham for services, she told him about me.

After Sunday School was over and morning service had started, the pastor called me up to the pulpit to sing. I had never been so frightened in my life! There I was, all dressed up in my floral dress, complete with ruffles. Those ruffles didn't quite cover my shaking knees, though. I was so small they had to stand me on a chair so I could be seen.

Then I started to sing:

"Like the ship that's tossed, driven and battered by an angry sea;
When the storms of life are raging and the ferry falls on me . . ."

Before I realized what was happening, the church became very emotional. People were crying. Some of the people had to be carried out. I thought they were dead! They had been slain in the Spirit. I was scared to death!

I was about 5 1/2 when I started my singing career. My sister and I started harmonizing together and we would sing all the time. I'm sure we got on our family's nerves because my mother used to call out, "Be quiet!" when everyone was in bed trying to sleep. But we would sing until we fell asleep.

We had no television and we barely had a radio. The one we had was battery-operated and most of the time it didn't work. When it did, we would hear Ernest Tubb, Tennessee Ernie Ford, Hank Williams, and Eddy Arnold. When it didn't work, we'd sing to keep busy.

We could also pick up a black station out of Birmingham, Alabama, "WEDR," and we would hear gospel singers like Mahalia Jackson, Harmonizing Four, and The Davis Sisters. We also listened to the blues singers like B.B. King, Ruth Brown, and many others. I had a love between country, gospel and rhythm & blues. I think that is how I developed my style.

We got so good our pastor began to take us to other churches. By the time I was eight years old, we had started a quartet with two other girls in our neighborhood. We called ourselves The Four Golden Echoes: consisting of my sister Maggie, Leatha Mae Malcolm, Betty Jean Byars, and myself. We became rather famous on a small scale. People would come from miles around to hear us sing.

We didn't get much money, but we were always invited to dinner after the concerts, and dinner was always a treat. We'd sing thinking of chicken drumsticks, biscuits, gravy and chocolate cake. We couldn't wait to sink our teeth into that southern-fried chicken the church people would prepare! We would take home the money we earned from our singing and help Mama support the family.

Mama was one of the sweetest, kindest people I have ever known. She had a heart of pure gold, and she really loved the Lord. She was born and raised in Alabama, and both her mother and father were farmers. She never had much schooling; just enough to learn how to read and write. She married my father when she was thirteen years old. Six years later, my older brother, Sam, was born. His twin brother died at birth. After that, came my brother, Joe, sister, Polly (who died when she was nine years old), Lillie, Maggie, me and my brother, Robert.

We were very poor. Even though Mama was unable to dress us properly, that never stopped her from taking us to church. My mother couldn't dress us like the other mothers dressed their little girls, but she tried. She used to make our dresses out of fertilizer sack material. She could sew pretty-well, and sometimes the material would be in floral designs and rather attractive patterns! Mama would make our panties and slips out of white flour-sack material. After she soaked the flour out of it, she would bleach it white. Well, almost. There would still be writing on the flour sacks. Sometimes it would all come off, and sometimes it wouldn't.

I remember a fight I was in one day after school. As the girl and I tumbled on the ground, my dress came up and right down the back side of my panties were big red letters: "Self-Rising." The kids laughed so hard, the fight was over. I cried. I was so embarrassed. But these kinds of incidents were very common in our small community. Most of us were from very low-income families. I always prayed and asked God, "Please let us live like other people." We made it only by the grace of God.

We used to call our house "air conditioned" because the air would come in through the planks on the floor in winter. As we looked down we could see chickens walking underneath the house .

It could get very cold in winter. My two sisters and I used to sleep together under about five quilts. When we turned over, all the quilts would fall on the floor, but somehow we survived. We would wake up, get up and put the cover back on us again and go back to sleep.

Though we didn't have much, Mama shared what we had with those in need. She would give drunks a bed for the night and a stray kitten or puppy a meal. She seemed to have a special love for all of the world's outcasts. I saw her get out of bed on a cold night, make a fire in the stove, and cook a meal for hungry strangers passing through. People would talk about her and say, "Mrs. Rosa is going to get it one day if she continues to do that," but she never did. When I think about it now, Mama reminds me so much of Jesus.

She passed away in March of 1979. I miss her warmth. No one was quite like her. I never remember her talking bad about anyone. She would tell us to just "pray for them." I used to say, "Mama, I can't do that," and she would say, "Oh, yes you can!" It would be some years before I knew exactly what she meant. The love of Jesus in your heart will cause you to do that. Mama used to pray a lot, especially when she was cooking and cleaning. Sometimes she would also fast before the Lord. I watched her all the time.

I would often see her cry, too. Mama would try to hide her tears from me and she would send me outside to play. She had to be sad, because I know she wanted the best for us, but she couldn't give it to us because she had no help from my father. That's because he was a drunk. There's really no other way to say it. Mama had to have the love of Jesus to put up with him.

My father was a hard-worker, though. He worked both our farm and the coal mines. He made a good salary according to the times, but he had a drinking problem and a gambling problem too. If my mother didn't go to his job on Fridays to collect his paycheck, we saw none of his money. If he didn't drink it up, he would gamble it away. My father was real moody and quiet until he got drunk. Then, he became all mouth — quite a comedian, in-fact. We used to laugh at everything he did then. But he could get really embarrassing.

He used to invite all of his drinking buddies over to our house and force my sister and me to sing. Then he would take off his hat and pass it around and collect an offering! All of his friends were drinking, so they would give real good tips. Then Daddy would take the money and buy more booze.

He would get drunk and sleep in the ditches by the roadside. When he woke up, he smelled so bad that even the cats would leave home when Daddy stumbled into the house. That's when he would want to pick us up and set us on his knees, but I was the only one who would let him do it. He reeked of alcohol.

My father hated church as much as my mother loved it. He used to say, "All preachers are phonies," and "There is no God." He would even curse the thunder and lightening in stormy weather. We were afraid to be in the same room with him when it was storming, fearing God would strike him down at any second. But, God never did. He is so merciful. You should have seen us running when daddy started to curse God!

One week our Church held a revival and Daddy told my mother not to go but she dressed and went anyway. He had been drinking, so he followed us to church.

It was a typically hot Alabama summer day and even more sweltering inside where nearly 75 people gathered for the Friday evening service. The cardboard funeral home fans flipped back and forth as the churchgoers sought a bit of relief from the heat.

Daddy sat down in the back of the church. He looked bad and smelled even worse. But he was good . . . until the preacher started to preach.

That's when Daddy got started. Everything the preacher said, Daddy would answer, "Yeah, preacher!" real loudly and sarcastically. If the preacher said "sinner," Daddy would answer, "And you another one, hypocrite, yeah, another one." Then he yelled from the very back pew, "Preacher, you sin, too. I saw you the other night. You thought I didn't see you, didn't you?"

I could hear my Mama say, "Oh my God! I don't believe this!" People were snickering and whispering. Finally, the deacons had to throw him out.

I was sitting with my girlfriends and all of my friends looked at me, grinning. I could have crawled through the floor. I was so embarrassed.

It took my poor mother a long time to hold her head up in the community again. But through it all, she kept dragging us to church.

Chapter 2

A Time Of Discovery

As early as I can remember, I disliked my father because he caused most of our pain and humiliation. I felt like that until I was about 10 years old.

My oldest brother, Sam, was then 19. He had taken all he could stand of my father's behavior. My two cousins, who lived in Cleveland, Ohio, had written and invited Sam to move there. They were sure they could find him a job, so he decided to leave.

We went down to the Blue & Gray Drugstore on Hanceville's Main Street that hot fall day to wait with him for the bus which would take him to Cleveland. I cried myself sick when he got on that bus because Sam was the only father figure in our home. He had quit school to work for other farmers to help my mother support us. I respected and loved him so much. So when he left I didn't know what we were going to do.

As soon as he got to Cleveland he found a good job working in a steel plant. He wrote Mama about a young lady with whom he had fallen in love and two months later they were married. He bought a home in Twinsburg, Ohio, a suburb about 30 minutes outside of Cleveland, Ohio, and wrote to find out if we wanted to move there.

My mother agreed and he sent money for transportation. I was so happy, I couldn't sleep the night before we left. I couldn't imagine waking up without hearing roosters, hens, cows, and mules. The idea of not hearing those farm noises made me shiver with excitement. I'd had my fill of those sounds.

I got up at 4 o'clock that morning. I just couldn't sleep. I was too excited imagining how Cleveland would be!

We left at about 7 o'clock for the bus station. I vividly remember the scene. It was October or November, but in Alabama it was still almost as hot as summer. My mother dressed Maggie and me in snowsuits and boots because she knew that Cleveland would be cold. We looked so ridiculous getting on that bus in Alabama! While everyone else wore summer clothing, we were dressed for winter!

I jumped up and down in my seat from excitement. I couldn't sit still because I was so anxious, fearing that at any minute Daddy would come to stop us. But he didn't.

When we finally got to Cleveland, it was snowing. I had never seen so much snow in my whole life. Now those boots and snowsuits didn't look so ridiculous! Sam and his new wife, Ethel, were waiting for us at the bus terminal. I was so happy to see Sam again.

My sister-in-law was a very religious person. "We go to church tomorrow night", she said as we were on the way to our new home, "and I want you girls to get ready and go with me. I want our overseer to hear you sing."

When we moved to Cleveland, we moved into an uptown life-style! We just didn't know what to do with all the convenience we encountered there. In Alabama, we used candles and kerosene lamps to light our home. But when we got to Cleveland there were electric lights. I can still remember my sister, Maggie, trying to put those electric lights out on our first night there! She blew at the bulb, looked at it still lit, and blew again!

"What in the world are you doing?" my sister-in-law asked her when she came in and saw Maggie blowing.

"Trying to blow the lights out!" she answered, puzzled. No one had told her that the electric lights were turned off by pulling a chain instead! We must have laughed for a few hours about it.

We had an equally interesting adventure when we discovered the flush commode. Needless to say, we hadn't ever used one. It was one of those that had the chain you pulled to flush it. We were so frightened of that noise, it was a big monster to us. We left the door wide open so that when we left the bathroom we could make a quick getaway down the hall.

One time Sam sent my sister and me to the store on the corner to get some white potatoes. Being from the South, we didn't speak as people from Ohio did. Our accent was country. We called potatoes "taters!" and we called paper bags "pokes!" So my sister and I skipped around to the store and said "We wan' sum taters an' a poke ta put 'em in!"

The store owner tried to understand what we said. He drilled us about 10 minutes and still he couldn't understand. He picked up the phone and called Sam and they had the biggest laugh. That was just one of many such incidents.

Tuesday night finally came, and we went to the church. It was the same kind of church that had come to our house to conduct a revival, only a lot better. They had a full band—bass, drums, guitar, keyboards, and steel guitar. I had never heard such beautiful music! When they stopped to take an offering, they called on different ones to sing or play or use whatever talents they had. Finally, the master of ceremony called on us.

"We have two little girls from Alabama! Let's give them a hand." We were on!

We started to sing and the entire church stood up and started clapping, shouting, and cheering. Oh my, were they excited!

When the service was over, the overseer called us to her office. She was the biggest woman I had ever seen. She was 6 foot 3 inches tall and must have weighed 300 pounds.

This woman had churches everywhere, and she even had a school in Nashville. She asked my sister-in-law if we could attend. I liked the idea very much because I didn't like the schools in Cleveland. I never liked fighting but I had to fight everyday. I was ready to leave the school after only a week. I ran home every day, leaving a trail of books behind me. My mother forced me to go back and pick up my homework papers, which were strewn along the street because I had been in such a hurry to get home.

I was a country girl to those city kids. They made fun of the way I talked, dressed, and everything else about me. We really began to pressure our mother to let us go to Nashville.

"You are too young to be leaving home," she responded.

Oh how we pleaded! She never said no but she never said yes either. During the time she was making up her mind, my father came to Cleveland. He was good for two weeks. He found a job in a laundromat and brought his money home for those two weeks. Then he slipped back into his old behavior pattern. My mother got so disgusted with him, she said to us, "Go on to Nashville. I'm sure that lady can do more for you than I can." We were excited, not knowing what to expect. But anything was better than home.

When we arrived in Nashville, I saw all of these beautiful buildings . . . picturesque college campuses. Nashville was a beautiful city. When we finally arrived at our school, I'd never seen lawns more perfect, except in story books. There was a big house, as large as a mansion, where the overseer lived, another big building where the school was, and a big dormitory. It was exciting to meet kids from all parts of the country at one time, Detroit, Chicago, Los Angeles, and New York. Oh, I thought I was in heaven! No more outdoor toilets, no more kerosene lamps! All the modern conveniences!

After three months, my sister and I would sometimes sing at the daily prayer services in the chapel. That was the rule, chapel every day. Maggie and I were working our way up. While we were singing one day after school, the overseer's granddaughter came in. We encouraged her to sing with us, because we figured that would be a good way to receive favor from the overseer. She was a little shy, but we kept complementing her until she finally started to sing. We sounded good as a trio.

We called the overseer and sang a song to her. She became very excited, but only because of her granddaughter. We started rehearsing every day, and got to be pretty good. So good that we started going on church crusades with the overseer.

A year later, we made our first record and continued traveling. I finally got a chance to see the world. The overseer had about 50 churches in different parts of the country and outside the U.S. including Nassau and Cuba. There was one in Los Angeles, New York, Detroit, Cleveland, Cincinnati, and Toledo, just to name a few.

We became so well known that people wanted more records. Our manager negotiated a contract with Nashboro Records — we were moving into the big time. We started to do concerts with famous gospel groups. We sang with Sam Cooke and The Soul Stirrers, Aretha and C. L. Franklin, The Staple Singers, The Davis Sisters, The Ward Singers, Mahalia Jackson, The Blind Boys of Alabama and Mississippi, Paul Roberson, and Lou Rawls, when he was with the Pilgrim Travelers.

We now had radio airplay, and our records began to sell. Needless to say, we were going commercial. In the beginning, we sang exclusively in our churches to pay for our tuition. Then the purpose began to change. There was lots of money being made, but we weren't getting any. My mother didn't know anything about the business and my father was an alcoholic, so we were taken advantage of.

Instead of receiving our intended education, we began traveling every day, staying on the road more than we stayed in school. We slept in station wagons and cars. Ironically, the more money we made for the organization, the worse we were treated. They began to neglect us. They even stopped feeding us properly.

We would travel all night and wake up in the morning standing in the yard of a grocery store. Someone bought us potted meat and crackers, sardines, peanut butter, jelly, and things like that. We nibbled on it all day. Sometimes I would be so hungry I would cry. My sister held me in her arms saying, "It's going to be all right."

I was only 14 years old at the time. No sleep,... no vitamins,... no school,... nothing. I was miserable. The only thing that kept us going was the fact that we were "famous." We loved the applause, the crowds, and we loved being accepted for the first time in our lives. By the time we arrived at the auditorium, we discovered people had waited to see us. That made us happy

Meanwhile Mavis, Pops, Cleo and Pervis Staples became our close friends. They knew of our situation because I had confided in them. So, Mavis and Pervis started to share some of their money with us. Pervis would send me $5.00 or sometimes $10.00 and that would make me so happy. Money stretched a long, long way in the 50s. I loved all the gospel singers I traveled with. They became my family.

Segregation was a real problem in the 50s and black gospel singers had to travel in caravans. It just wasn't safe for one car of blacks to travel alone. It wasn't unusual for a car of so-called "cops" to stop and heckle you and make you get out of the car. If you said you were singers they would make you sing and dance for them until they were satisfied. Then, they would let you go, hopefully.

We were not allowed to stay in nice hotels and motels then. Special houses were prepared for us when we came into a city. Although there were some black hotels, most of them were not in good condition. In some cities, we had no other choice than to stay in them, and fight roaches and mosquitoes all night after traveling for days. We were so tired we could hardly rest. As if that wasn't enough, four people sometimes had to sleep in one bed.

I grew to know all of the popular gospel singers very well. Traveling together, as we did, we would often stop for gas and ride in each other's cars. I was especially fond of Sam Cooke. We would sit and talk for hours. I remember telling him how I disliked the conditions we lived under and he was very sympathetic.

Later, I learned he was thinking of going to the "other side" to sing pop music. That really bothered me knowing how badly people treated gospel singers who "crossed over." You were never welcomed back into gospel. I hated to see that happen to Sam but he assured me that he knew some people who had control of that field and nothing bad would happen.

Lou Rawls and I met when I was singing and he liked me right away. We started to date. I was 17 then and I ran away from the Jewels so I could marry Lou, but his mom talked me out of it. She said her son was still "wild" and advised me to go back and finish my education. That was the best advice I ever received because we were not ready for marriage. Sometimes Lou and I would get to the high school auditorium [where we performed] too early. Then we'd find a "soul food joint", eat a good meal, then go back and play ball for an hour or two. That was fun.

I met Aretha Franklin and her father - Rev. C. L. Franklin and we became friends. I liked Aretha. She was a talented singer and was in our age group. I also loved to talk to Clara Ward and her singers. They gave us good advice — teaching us how to be well-behaved young ladies, which I appreciated. Everyone in the different groups gave us tips on growing up.

The Davis Sisters from Philadelphia were also close to us. I especially liked Thelma because she was so motherly. Ruth was one of the world's greatest singers in my opinion. When we visited them in Philadelphia, Thelma would always fix us dinner. Curtis, their keyboard player, was extraordinarily talented and he taught me chords on the piano. The little playing I do now is because of Curtis.

I remember when I first met Mahalia Jackson, I thought she was a famous queen. I was outside of her dressing room door at the Grand Ole Opry House in Nashville, Tennessee. Her pianist came up and said "Hi little girl, what's your name?" I told her. She asked if I would like to meet Mahalia, and when I said, "Yes." she told me to follow her. I went into her room speechless. Mahalia spoke to me. I was so nervous I can't remember a word she said but I do remember she kissed me on my cheek. She couldn't believe I could sing and was very surprised when she heard me later that night. I was 14 years old when I met Mahalia. We did a lot of concerts with her after that but I will forever cherish that moment in Nashville.

Everyone agreed that we were the most talented girls in our day. They had no idea how miserable our lives were. We worked hard but we received nothing... not even spending change... not even a dime for a Coke. We needed lots of clothes because of our busy travel schedule, but our administrator refused to buy us clothes. We didn't need stage clothes because we wore robes. But we hardly had any everyday clothes, and I was miserable. My sister and I thought of an idea. Let's steal!

During intermission we went to the auditorium and sold black-and-white glossy pictures of the singing groups. We secretly kept half of the money. With that money we pocketed we bought material. Our mother had taught us how to sew and we made our skirts and shirts while traveling. That soon ended. We found out that the group members could count! They counted the pictures and discovered what we'd done. Bishop Jewel threatened to whip us if we didn't stop. I didn't want to get a whipping because she would beat us with raw hides, so we stopped.

Meanwhile, the granddaughter and great-granddaughter went shopping at Sak's Fifth Avenue and other expensive stores. When we were in Los Angeles, they shopped in Beverly Hills. I used to get so jealous. I thought about returning home, but when I thought of my father, I quickly changed my mind. At least we were famous. Everyone looked at us as stars. Only a few people knew the real story.

That is when I began to hate church and religion. I thought God was a bad God. We sang for Him everyday, yet look at how we were treated! "I thought you had no respect of persons," I'd say to God. I used to think, "If you are God, and you really do exist, then stop these people from mistreating us." He never did. Needless to say, I was confused. Though I didn't know it at the time, it wasn't God mistreating us. It was people who had "religion" but not a relationship with Jesus. Therefore, they lacked real love.

One incident I'll always remember. I was 13. We worked our way to California, by doing concerts. At one point, traveling through the hot desert, my tooth began to ache so badly I thought I would go out of my mind. I tried to stop the pain by taking many aspirins. At night, during the concerts, the pain wasn't so bad, as long as I was singing. As soon as I relaxed, I would go crazy with pain.

I thought we would never get to Los Angeles. I just knew when we got there, I would be allowed to have my tooth extracted. No such luck.

When we arrived a program was scheduled the next night at a church. There we met a lady I'll always remember. I'll call her Lisa. She really liked me. She and her mother were very wealthy.

After the program that night I thought my toothache would kill me. A friend of ours, also another singer on the tour, tried to help me by putting pressure on the nerve of my aching tooth all night. She hoped I would fall asleep. I couldn't, instead I cried all night.

The next morning the overseer called me into her bedroom. Fear built up as I walked in. She was propped up in her bed, covered with beautiful sheets like some movie star.

"I'm going to make your toothache stop," she said. Someone told her if you put devil's lye in a cavity it would eat up the decay and stop the hurting. She said, "Come here girl and get on your knees." I obeyed because I wanted the pain to stop.

"The toothache will be gone in a little while," she said. She put two grains of lye in the cavity, put cotton on top, and told me to bite down and hold it there.

I did, and oh my Lord! The lye began to do its damage. It began to eat the cavity, true enough, but also my tongue, my lips, and my throat. I jumped up and ran to the bathroom in tears, I was in more pain than I can ever remember in my life. The pain was so tremendous I wanted to black out. How I hurt!

The lady that held my hand all night mentioned the horrible experience to Lisa as they casually spoke on the phone the next morning. After they hung up, Lisa called the Los Angeles Police Department, asking them to investigate a child abuse case. Later that evening the police came. They knocked on the door and demanded "Open up!" The tour people quickly escorted us to the back bedroom. They told us to say nothing was wrong to the police and that they must be mistaken. My tooth still hurt. There were tears in our eyes and fear in our minds. In her living room, the overseer explained to the police what good care she took of us. She talked about the school for needy children in Nashville, and that she was truly a woman of God who wouldn't think of mistreating innocent children. Well, she convinced the police. The police questioned us but we had been commanded to lie. They left.

Nobody said very much but the following morning the granddaughter got me up early.

"Get dressed. We are going to the dentist," she said.

She took me to a Pediatric Dentist, the best in Beverly Hills, who put me to sleep and extracted the tooth, I felt no pain! The following day, they took us shopping and bought us quite a few clothes. This good treatment lasted for a little while. I think the experience scared them into a change of behavior. The officer had asked them about our schooling and told them what happens to adults who mistreat children.

When we got back to Nashville, the tour people started looking for a tutor to travel with us so we wouldn't miss any school. Our new teacher went on the road with us. He insisted we have three meals a day. Even if we were running late, they just had to wait. He said, "My students won't be able to learn without proper diets." He really fought hard for us. His name was James Peebles. He had just graduated from college and was a very smart young teacher. The bishop hired him right away. He made a real difference in our lives. Things changed for the better for us. He made sure we were not over-worked or under-fed because we were still developing young ladies. We really did appreciate him. He later published the original African Heritage Bible.

Chapter 3

God Is Real!

By the time we stopped touring, my mother had moved back to our farm in Alabama. When I went back home, my father had passed away and, sad as it may seem, things were much better without him.

I was so used to traveling and being in so many different cities that the country was rather difficult to adjust to again. But, I had to try. I was so restless. I wanted to continue to travel and sing. I even thought of going solo, but instead I settled down and finished school.

During my senior year of high school, I started dating a young man. He was the only one in our area who had a nice car. So, at the very least I had wheels to get around. I liked him only enough to keep from being bored. We went to the movies, to dances, on joy rides, and so on. He began to get serious. I teased him to keep him interested but I was just leading him on. I went wild. We'd go drinking, cruising, smoking, parking, and hanging out late. One night I went too far. Six weeks later I discovered I was pregnant. I didn't want a baby. I thought of having an abortion but they weren't easy to get in 1959. I was miserable. What was I going to do? How would I tell Mama? It was four months before I told her. Then she and I cried together. We became closer than ever. She asked me what I wanted to do and I said I didn't know. My boyfriend, Joe, wanted to get married and I didn't.

School would end in two months, so I continued with my education and graduated. Three weeks after my son, Marcel, was born, Joe and I were married and moved in with his family. I wasn't ready for marriage but, for the sake of my son, I did it anyway. I settled into my new life of being a mother and a wife.

Joe's father was a holiness preacher. He had a church a few miles from home. I was there only a month before I began feeling guilty about not going to church, so I went with them. He preached fire and brimstone and I began to worry about my "sinful" life.

The church had no music — just tambourines and people's hands to clap and I really wanted to help. I knew I could play the piano but I wasn't "sanctified" so I wasn't "fit."

One night at church, I decided to get "fit." I tarried, called on Jesus until I foamed at the mouth. "Boy, do you have to work hard to get Jesus!" I thought. "My Lord, He is so hard to get!" I went on like that, until finally I got tired and started to say anything I could muster up. They said, "She's got it! She's got it!" "If you say so," I thought.

I didn't know then that that's not the way you get Jesus in your life. It's not by works, lest any man should boast, but it's a gift (Ephesians 2:8,9). You don't have to work for a gift, it's freely given to you. You just ask Him by faith into your life, and He comes in and makes His home within you. If only I had known that then. Anyway, I got the "ghost." I don't know how holy it was, though! I started to play for the church. I formed a choir and we became pretty good.

Meanwhile, my husband, who had always been jealous, was getting more and more jealous. He became so possessive, it was difficult to live with him. He accused me of messing around with everyone, even his own brother. My life was miserable once again.

I played for the church choir, and that kept me busy. I was pregnant again, too. When Marcel was fourteen months old, I had another son, Marcus. Two years after that I had my third son, Terry, and then three years later a daughter, Cassandra. When my daughter was eighteen months old, I had taken all I could stand of Joe's unusual jealousy. He literally kept me barefoot and pregnant for seven years.

My father-in-law's ministry was based on divine healing. He preached on it all the time, and there were indeed a few miracles that took place in our body of believers. They did not believe in doctors; they believed God could heal any sickness or disease. I believe He can, too, but this gift works by love. Without the love of God it's merely another religion. Every time Jesus healed someone, he said, "YOUR faith has made you whole." These church people believed if any member went to a doctor, it was a reproach on the church, especially on the preacher. People would become extremely sick and be in pain, but they would rather suffer than bring a reproach to their church.

Yet one experience proved to me that God can and does heal. We lived in Warrior, Alabama at the time. It was Sunday evening, after morning service and dinner. We were to have a radio broadcast at 4 P.M. Sunday. I was dressing, getting ready to go. "I'm going to pick up the other members," my husband said.

"Okay," I replied. Then I turned to my two-year-old son, Terry, and said, "Go with your daddy," who had already gone through the door and out to the car. My husband was unaware that Terry had followed him. When Joe started the car and backed up, he felt a "thump" beneath the wheels. His first thought was that the family dog had been hit. But, it wasn't. Little Terry had been right in the center of the back bumper and was knocked down and dragged underneath the car for about 10 feet over the hard, rutted, Alabama clay-dirt beneath. An 18 year-old boy who lived across the street from us began to shout, and he ran over to help. My husband stopped and I came out just in time to see this young man, with supernatural strength, lift up the car enough to pull Terry out.

I looked at my little boy. I couldn't believe my eyes. All the skin on the right side of his face was torn off and his back was injured. I tried to stand him on his feet to see if he could stand, but he couldn't. His back was moving and unstable. He crumpled to the ground, silent and in shock. I believe his back was broken. We took him in the house and laid him on the bed. He tried to get up, pulling himself up by his elbows, but his hips would fall from one side to the other. "Oh, God, please help me," I cried, as I held my injured baby. All of a sudden, I felt a peace come over me. "Let's go to the broadcast," I said. "God's going to heal Terry."

I wrapped him up in a blanket and had one of the church mothers take care of him while I went to play the piano for the broadcast. I just knew God was going to work a miracle. Faith is fantastic! It's not you operating, it's God. We did the broadcast, and nothing happened. They prayed. Still nothing happened. When we got home, Terry was hurting bad. The entire church came over after the broadcast and began praying and singing songs. But nothing happened. Yet I knew beyond a shadow of a doubt he was healed. I just believed!

Everyone left and went home. There I was, at the house, alone with my family, and Terry was still in pain. At 3 P.M.. he got worse and the pain became so intense that it was unbearable. Though I had read the Bible off and on, I hadn't really studied the Word of God for myself. I hadn't really paid attention. But, in this moment of trauma, I remembered a verse which the pastor had repeated many times with conviction, "If there be any sick among you, call for the elders." (James 5:14). I jumped up and put on my coat and ran to get the pastor.

He came over, and our faith was ripe enough to see a miracle. He sat Terry upon his knees, laid his hands on the boy's back, and prayed a prayer of faith. "Be healed!" the pastor finally shouted quite abruptly, startling some of us as we sat there. I saw a flash of light as the pastor laid hands on Terry's back.

"Get down and go to your momma," the pastor said. Terry jumped out of the pastor's lap and ran to me healed!

I put him back to bed and when I got him up a few short hours later that morning, new skin had grown on his face as though nothing had happened! He was healed! That miracle has stayed with me all of my life. The whole town came over the next day to get a look at Terry and that next Sunday we didn't have room in our church to hold everybody. Truly they had seen a miracle! Terry went into the Navy several years later. The Navy doctor said to

Terry, after looking at some of his X-rays, "What doctor set your collar bone back? Whoever he was, he did a perfect job."

I stayed in the church two more years. Later, when I went into secular music, I know God knew where I was headed. He never wanted me to forget that His power was real.

After Terry's healing, though, things weren't so good. I got to be very religious. I found myself pleasing people instead of pleasing God.

The people in our church didn't believe in televisions, either. It was a sin to have one. I invited my sister-in-law to move in with me after my brother left to serve in Vietnam. She accepted and brought her TV with her. The pastor heard about it and demanded I get rid of the set.

"It's not mine," I argued.

"Get it out of your house," he demanded.

When I refused to get rid of my sister-in-law's TV, he threw me out of the church. Some vacuum cleaner and insurance salesmen do a better job representing their companies than some people represent Jesus. That's why so many sinners never find the way because everybody has an idea how to get to heaven. One hundred different people are pointing in one hundred different directions. The poor sinner is confused. There is only one way, and nobody can get to the Father but by Jesus Christ. HE is the way. It's a relationship, not a religion!

"Okay, Lord," I said. "This is it. I'm through with churches, preachers, saints, and religious nuts. I'm through! There is another way, and I'm going to find it." You see, I had been in churches all of my life. I didn't know anything about the world. I had always been so sheltered. In order for me to reach "the world" I had to be trained. It was not His perfect will for me to become a part of the world, though He protected me through it all. Now I know how the world thinks, how they react to certain situations. I have felt depression, guilt, and sorrow. I have experienced alcoholism and the drug world. I became all of these things. Now I can reach out to those who need help. I know how to love the unlovely because I, too, have been unlovely.

Chapter 4

There's Life After Divorce

After being put out of church, I started to desire the things of the world. Having been in and around churches all of my life, I was not prepared for the world and the life I was to find. I was trusting, and I had a love for people. I was a softie, and that's a no-no in show biz.

I also wanted to be a star. I wanted to sing the blues. I was tired of being used by churches, and now it was time for me to earn some money. However, I never dreamed a country girl like me would reach the heights I reached in the entertainment world.

My oldest brother, Sam, moved back to Alabama. He heard me talking about singing secular songs. "It's about time you started thinking about yourself, Candi. Come and go with me Saturday night," he said.

He took me to a club in Birmingham called the 2728 Club. It held about 150 people and the place was packed. My brother and the club owner were good friends.

"Hey, O.J.!" he said. "Let my sister sing."

"No, man!" O.J. replied. "What if she can't sing?"

"Man, if she couldn't sing," Sam answered back, "I wouldn't be asking you to let her!"

O.J. looked at me and said, "Girl, you better not embarrass me." He got up to the mike and announced, "I have a surprise for you." (He had his fingers crossed!) "This girl is going to blow you away tonight. Let's hear it from Candi Staton!"

I sang, "If You Want a Do-Right Woman, You've Got to Be a Do-Right Man," an old Aretha Franklin favorite. I got a standing ovation. They were screaming, "More! More! More!" I didn't know another song, so I sang the same one again. After the performance, I went back to my seat and O.J. came over and asked "Do you want a regular job?" I told him, "Yes, I would love to work here." So I started working on Friday, Saturday, and Sunday nights.

I went to the record shop and bought every popular song that was on the market and learned them. Now I was ready. I worked in the club for about a month. By then, my husband had grown insanely jealous. He carried a gun whenever he came to pick me up. I knew I would never be a star as long as he was involved in my life.

A popular singer, Clarence Carter, came to the club about six weeks after I started. He and O.J. were good friends. O.J. asked Clarence if it was okay to let "my girl sing." Clarence approved, so I opened the show for him. The club went wild as usual, and so did Clarence. He even invited me to go on the road with him but I couldn't go because I had my kids and a very jealous husband.

Two months later, my husband and I separated. We had a fight, the worst experience of my life and it led to my first divorce. He had started drinking and smoking marijuana. One night he came home about midnight, and dumped me and my 18- month- old daughter, Cassandra, out of bed. He literally turned the bed over on us. I thought a tornado had hit. We crawled out from underneath the bed. He accused me of having an affair with a local deejay. Joe was in such a rage that he couldn't control himself. He started to hit me until I was black and blue. He tried to force me into the car saying he would drive me to my mother's house. I knew if I got into the car I wouldn't live. I just knew he intended to kill me.

He dragged me to the car and I fought all the way. I broke away and ran into the house. He caught me and dragged me out again. I pulled every piece of furniture I could to the door trying to hold on to something. Finally I grabbed the keys and tossed them into the shrubbery. As he looked for them, I ran next door, phoned my mother and step-father, who lived on a farm 30 miles away, to come get me. Joe didn't let me pack. He just dumped all of our things in the back of a manure stained truck bed and that's how I went back home to Mama. I stayed with her for about three months. My brother, Joe, who lived in Cleveland, invited me to live with him until I could find a job. I took all my kids except Terry who stayed with my mom.

Soon I got a job working as a nurse's assistant in a local hospital, and I began thinking seriously about being a nurse. My brother's home was small and my kids and his kids couldn't get along, so I moved in with my oldest sister Lillie. But the apartment owner said I couldn't stay there. What was I going to do? I started searching for an apartment. The only one I could afford was on the worst side of Cleveland. The rent was $65.00 a month, which resulted in another problem! "Who is going to keep the kids?" A co-worker at the hospital offered his support. He suggested moving into my apartment, on the condition that he would keep the kids at night. He worked a day-shift. Because of my upbringing, I did not want this man living with me but I had no choice. He moved in. I regretted it the first week. He left the kids alone and came and went as he willed. I knew I had to find another way, this wasn't working.

One weekend I visited a nightclub, I knew the drummer and he asked me sing. I was immediately hired. Now I worked two jobs, the hospital during the day and the nightclub at night. The money was better but the kids were still alone. I was about to give up and move back to Alabama.

My sister Maggie and her husband, James, had lived in Spain. James studied at the University of Spain for two years to earn a doctorate in foreign languages. Maggie and I were very close. She came to Cleveland looking for me after hearing about my plight. When she found me she couldn't believe how I lived. We started planning on how to get me out of that mess. Each child was placed in the home of a relative until I could get on my feet. My aunt took one child, my cousin took another, the kids' grandfather took one, and I kept the baby. We decided to move back to Nashville with my sister. The plan also called for me to go to nursing school, become a nurse, then take my kids back and properly raise them. I went back to Nashville and studied nursing.

About the time I was to register for school, Clarence Carter came through with his show for a big concert. My sister and I went to the concert. I could hardly wait to go backstage to see Clarence. I flirted my way through security and Clarence was pleased to see me. I asked him if he still needed someone to open his show.

"When can you start?" he asked.

"Now!" I answered.

It had worked out perfectly. All the kids were in good homes. I was free to go. "No responsibilities!" I thought, and go I did. One week later, I boarded a plane to go and join the CLARENCE CARTER Show. I was so excited! I could hardly sleep, thinking of what my future might hold.

When I got to the location of Clarence's next show, I had a good talk with him and explained my position. I told him I wasn't going to "go through" the band. That was a common practice when a new girl came to a band. In order to be accepted, she must sleep with each of the guys. It made the band feel at ease around her. Then they wouldn't have to respect her. They could say whatever they wanted to in the girl's presence. Clarence laughed, but he respected me for my stand. "Don't worry," he said. "You won't be expected to do that. I hired you to sing. Just tell me if anyone approaches you like that and I'll fire them." That sounded good to me!

I did my first non-gospel show of my life with the band and I was terrible! I didn't realize that "show business" means you have to put on a "show." I didn't know how. I was so used to being sincere when I sang gospel songs. Boy, this was different! The audience just looked at me; no expressions, just blank looks. I got through the first song and started to sing the second. They began to boo me. I couldn't believe that I was getting booed. Finally, I couldn't stand it any longer. I ran to the dressing room crying. Clarence came my dressing room and said, "Okay... I know what I'm going to have to do. I'm going to teach you how to do a show." And boy, did he teach me! We rehearsed all day the next day and that night I was better.

Popular singer Jerry Butler came to one show we did in Miami. He pulled me to the side and gave me lots of pointers. I also watched Sly Stone when Clarence was in a show with him at Fillmore East in New York. I learned fast. When I sang in churches, I looked up and held my hands together. I did the same thing in the clubs. No wonder the audience looked at me so strangely! I had to learn "body language," the sexual moves. So, I saw "blue" movies, picked up sex books . . . anything to teach me how to be sexy. Little by little my vocabulary changed. After a year, I cursed like a sailor. Each time I went on stage, I was determined to captivate my audience, and I did. Men screamed, and came toward the stage just to touch me. I wanted to remind them of their wildest fantasies. Women turned green with envy but I gave them something to think about. I knew I made progress.

After about two weeks with Clarence, he took me to see Rick Hall in Muscle Shoals, Alabama. He had already told Rick about me and he was anxious to meet me. I went into Rick's office.

"Clarence, she's pretty. But, are you sure she can sing?" Clarence laughed he didn't answered.

"Let's find a piano." We found one and I could play a little, so I got through "Do-Right Woman."

"Do you know another one?" Rick asked. "I produced that one for Aretha Franklin so I want to hear something original."

I had a little "pet" song, "To Hear You Say You're Mine," I wrote up, so I sang that. Rick was sold.

The following night we went into the studio and recorded three songs. Rick began to look for a "deal" for me with a big record company. Finally, about three months later, he called me "Guess what! Capitol Records is interested in you!"

We signed the deal two weeks later. A month later I had my first record on the market. The song was called "I'd Rather Be an Old Man's Sweetheart Than to Be a Young Man's Fool." It sold half a million copies. Capitol Records finally signed the deal with Rick Hall and Fame Records. I was their first artist. A star was born.

The company introduced me by putting together a seven-state tour entitled "Premiere A Star." Capitol did all of their artists like that. They invited all of the top deejays in every state we went to.

They had dinner, champagne, hundreds of people and I was the star. When I walked into the banquet hall, the cameras flashed. The press held interviews for Bill Board, Cash Box and Record World. Deejays conducted interviews with me to play on the air, and a big sound system blasted my single every night. As soon as the deejays left the party they started to play "I'd Rather Be an Old Man's Sweetheart" before anyone could eat their superb meal. They proposed a toast to me and I took the first sip of champagne. That's when I knew I liked the feeling it gave me and I stopped being nervous.

I could sell records! My life began to change drastically. Booking agencies phoned me. I stayed on the road with Clarence a little longer, I knew I would soon have to get a band and go solo, but, until then, I enjoyed traveling with Clarence.

He and I had grown fond of each other during all those days and nights traveling on the road from one show to another one. We learned quite a lot about each other. We would talk about our childhoods, and some incidents were so similar we would laugh for hours. The day would dawn without us having any sleep. Clarence and I became very good friends.

Clarence was not "good looking" in terms of what the world calls good looking and he was blind, but he had a good heart. He was awfully nice to me. Therefore, when we started to get serious about each other, everyone thought I wanted him for his money or for what he could do for me in show business. But it was not true, I fell in love with a good man. He was honest, he had depth, a sense of humor, an ability to converse, and he was well versed on every subject, politics, education, society, anything you might want to talk about. He always impressed me with his wit, especially when deejays interviewed him. The Clarence I met, fell in love with, later married and had a son with, was my idea of the best husband in the world. I planned to stay with him forever.

Chapter 5

Stand By Your Man?

Clarence and I married in 1970. It was a fabulous wedding. We rented a suite in the biggest hotel in Birmingham and one room for the wedding and reception. The Birmingham News, Billboard and Jet magazines were there. Many celebrities attended, including record people. Eddy Floyd ("Knock On Wood") supplied the entertainment for us. Champagne flowed. It went on until very early, or very late, depending on how you look at it. Rodgers Redding and Zelma Redding, Otis Redding's brother and widow attended. Rick Hall, my producer, and Capitol Records executives also attended. Clarence and I accomplished a lot together. He owned a restaurant, lots of property, and a home. I gave up my home (a mobile home I had parked by my mother's house so the kids could be together) and I moved in with him. We put a new den onto his house so the kids would have plenty of room, and we began our life together. I was so happy with him. By then I had a million-seller, "Stand By Your Man," and money was really coming in. Clarence had recorded three songs which became million-sellers for him, "Slip Away," "Too Weak to Fight," and "Patches."

All the girls in Clarence's hometown didn't like me because they had their eyes on "home boy." I used to get real nasty phone calls from the local girls, until Clarence finally decided to get us a private line. Our first and only baby was born in January of 1971. Clarence Carter Junior was a cute baby. Clarence was in Trinidad when the baby was born and I had been out of the hospital a week when my husband returned home. Clarence Junior was a fussy baby. He always had a cold and suffered from allergies. I never understood what was wrong with him until I had him tested for sickle cell anemia and found out he had a trait. After the baby was born, I suggested to Clarence to put our shows together so we could travel together. He refused and I wondered why. Then he started staying away from home more and more. It was as though he disliked coming home. Little by little I began to find out why.

I was doing a show in Akron, Ohio and after unloading the equipment, I was on my way to the dressing room when my guitar player stopped me. "Don't go in there. You take our dressing room," he said.

I was curious, so I stormed in. I looked around, and on the wall with the rest of the graffiti was a statement that said, "My name is Chiquita and I was here with my man Clarence on Jan. 1, 1972. I love him and he loves me."

I just stood there frozen. I couldn't believe that someone could be that stupid and bold at the same time.

"I told you not to come in here," Leroy reminded me.

I confronted Clarence with the graffiti when I got home. He denied it, so I sort of forgot about the incident. But, it wasn't long before I found out about his on going affair with his new female singer from North Carolina. She opened his show. In fact, she came to our house sat down and talked to me. I even gave her evening gowns to perform in. All the time, she was sleeping with my husband, and I didn't know it. The guys in the band knew but wouldn't tell me. During that time, I began to drink hard liquor. In fact, I began that night. I wasn't used to it and didn't like it much, though I did like the results. It helped me cope with the situation, so I thought.

We moved to Atlanta in 1972. We had a lovely home there. One day this singer came over to the house and we were all laughing and sipping champagne. Clarence was sitting between the two of us and the guys must have thought that was funny. I learned two weeks later why they had been laughing, and I thought I would die. I was hurt I so deeply could hardly bear it. I doubled over with pain.

I cried until there were no tears left. I begged Clarence to fire her. He flatly refused. "You won't run my business," he told me.

I left him, got the kids and went to Nashville. From there, I called him again.

"Please fire the girl," I begged. "If you do, I can forget about the whole thing."

But, he again refused. Instead, he invited me to leave if I couldn't take the situation.

I found a lawyer and began divorce proceedings. My lawyer found out the amount of property we had and all we would lose. He wanted to talk to us together and Clarence consented. Then he tried to talk us into staying together by convincing Clarence that it was more profitable to stay together than divorce. We decided to try it again.

The marriage was never the same. Clarence seemed to dislike me. We never talked and I missed that. He stayed down in the den until he was sure I was asleep, then he eased into bed. The reconciliation wasn't working, to say the least. He began to make financial demands on me for things he wanted. He even stopped working. So I ended up paying the bulk of the bills every month. Then Clarence even set a curfew for me to be home by. I couldn't take being treated like a 16 year-old.

One morning, I told him if we couldn't continue to live like we once did, then I was leaving for good. "I'm not going to be in at 11:00. I'm not going to meet any more of your demands. I'm through."

He calmly walked around the table with his coffee cup in hand, a smile on his face, as though he wanted to make up. He grabbed me and beat the living daylights out of me. I was bruised from head to toe . . . black eye, black arms. Here I was battered and bruised and I had a TV show to do the following day. I rushed out of the house, got in the car, and went over to a friend's house.

"What happened?" he asked. I told him and he advised me to call my lawyer. Don Weiserman is one of the best divorce attorneys in Atlanta.

"Come down here right now," Weiserman said.

He had a photographer take pictures of my bruises. I kept feeling dizzy, so I laid down for a while before I went back home. When I got there, Clarence acted as if nothing had happened. I went into the bedroom and began packing. I knew when I came back from the trip to North Carolina that I was leaving for good.

North Carolina turned out to be a successful weekend. I used heavy make-up to cover the bruises, and somehow I made it through. When I returned to Atlanta on Monday, I didn't go straight home. Instead, I went to the Guest Quarters in Atlanta to get a place to stay. I dropped off my suitcases, went to my house, and walked in through the garage into the den. Clarence was sitting there "watching" TV.

"I only came by to pick up some clothes," I told him. "I'm leaving you for good. You'll be hearing from my attorney." With that, he jumped up and started towards me.

"Oh no. Not again," I said and he turned away. I packed the car with everything I could stuff into it. Kids were riding on top of clothes. We looked a mess, leaving the neighborhood. Oh, he was so angry! He could have killed me, but he remained cool.

We had already filed income taxes for that year—a joint return. But when I left him he had his taxes done over and he destroyed all of my receipts. I was bound to get into trouble with the IRS. Sure enough, they contacted me and said I owed them $8,000 in back-taxes and social security payments. Clarence told them I had a band but had never reported it to them, and that I hadn't paid taxes or social security. I was hurt, disgusted, angry, and confused. I began to think, "How could someone do this to me? Someone I've lived with and had a child with?"

I felt I had taken all I could stand to take from life, so I made plans to end it all. I was tired of struggling. I went to the drugstore and had a prescription of sleeping pills refilled and I made a date with death. I called my mother and asked her to come and get my kids. I told her I needed time to rest and think about what I was going to do with my life. She came and we talked for three or four hours before she left. Then I was alone. I shall never forget that night. It was

Saturday night, about 9 o'clock I walked around and kept looking at those pills, thinking, "Do I really want to do this?" You know, the devil was there giving me all the good reasons why I should. So, I listened to him, and I took all 24 pills. Then I panicked.

"Oh, my God!" I said. "I'm going to die! I'm really going to die in a few minutes." I thought about calling the paramedics, but I decided, "No. I'll just suffer the consequences. I'll be better off. No more hurts, no more pain. No more nothing."

Then I began to cry out to God "Oh, God! I don't really want to die! Please save me! I'm sorry that I was so foolish to do what I just did. God, give me another chance to raise my kids." Then I saw something I'd never seen before. I saw the faces of all my kids pass before me. It was not like a mind picture, this was real—like on a screen. They all were smiling at me. Then I began to get sick. I ran to the bathroom, and all 24 sleeping pills came back up. I stood there, with tears streaming down my cheeks. I looked in the mirror and saw what a wreck I was.

"God, I sure do thank you for saving my life, even though I am not living for you," I said. He loved me enough to save me.

I hate divorces, because they take so much out of you. You lose so much of yourself. God hates them too, and He understands how you suffer. The children, if you have any, also suffer. That's why so many children are rebellious, filled with low self-esteem-and can't find direction, because of divorce.

I can't begin to describe the hurt and pain I felt. It is like someone takes your heart, misuses it, wounds it, breaks it and puts it back inside of your body. You cry but there is no relief. The pain won't go away. There is no real cure, except for the Blood of Jesus. He knows how to heal the broken hearted. I sat there all alone for a few minutes, just thinking. Then, I called a friend and told him that I had tried to kill myself and that I had taken 24 sleeping pills. "I'll be right there," he said before I could finish.

"Oh, well. I need the company anyway," I reasoned.

My friend came, and we sat and talked for a long time. He was afraid to leave me; he thought I was going to try suicide again. But I had done all the stupid stuff I was going to do in one night! So he left and I finally fell asleep.

God was watching over my life. He knew then that I would one day minister His Word in song. I couldn't see it. He knew he had to get me beyond religion and into a relationship with the person of Jesus Christ. It took a long time for me to see the light, the True Light. I was fed up with the church or anything that represented it. I didn't want anyone to talk to me about church, or God, or Jesus, but I knew deep inside they were real. How could I not believe, after experiencing that miracle with Terry. I knew God was real. However, I had only seen Him in people and they were poor representatives of Jesus.

I filed for divorce from Clarence and it was nasty. We really hurt each other. We both were trying to win a contest so we had to do everything we could to win. When it was all over, the judge ruled mostly in my favor. I got a sizable amount of money and so did the lawyers.

I was beginning to move into the right direction. I had already purchased a new house in Atlanta, and I was on my way to straightening out my life again. I began to think, "Well, if I can't kill myself, I'm going to live it up. I'm going to have a ball!" And that's just what I started to do.

Chapter 6

Everything That Shines Is Not Gold

"I have been there and I have seen them. This journey is not an easy one to travel, not as luxurious as it may seem. I only hope at the end of this journey I'll still have me."

I once quoted these words to myself sitting in a lonely hotel room. The road to the fame that I was seeking was often discouraging, even chaotic. There seemed to be an incredible number of road-blocks. The music industry sells to markets and each market is characterized by a certain style, pop, rock, jazz, rhythm & blues, country, gospel, etc. When you make your first record, you are looking for an audience. It doesn't matter who they are, just as long as they buy your records. If you are black, it is natural to appeal to your own race. If you do appeal to them, they become your foundational audience. Therefore, you make music to try and satisfy your record-buying audience. Many times we fall into a rut and we only sell to one audience. It is very different now. Since 1971, when I got started, the music industry has almost closed the gap between music types. After you establish your credibility as a record-selling artist, you may want to try your wings in other avenues of the music business.

The problem was, when I got started, if you made a "pop" song, the promotion men marched directly into the black radio stations. If it was real "white" sounding, the black deejays wouldn't play it because it didn't appeal to their listening audiences. The white jocks wouldn't play it because it's too "black" and the record company wouldn't spend that kind of money to promote pop. So, there you were with no sales, then the record company complains because you're not selling any records. You were forced to go back to "black music."

A lot of injustice exists in the music business, simply because you are black, but not to the same degree as in the past. There is prejudice on both sides. Black deejays won't play white records, and white deejays won't play black records. However, people are finally coming to the realization that music is music.

Even though the prejudice is finally beginning to melt away, some black entertainers still fall into what some people call the "Chitlin' Circuit." It is what the name implies. The chitterlings, or chitlin's, are the intestines of a hog. These "Chitlin' Circuit" gigs prostitute the artists' talents. The promoters get more entertainment for less money and in very deplorable conditions. Once you get into the circuit, it is very hard to get out because you are labeled.

You are booked in basically black clubs by promoters who still have a slave mentality. They try to book you around the first of the month, when the welfare checks come to the people in the community. That is the time of month when they get the largest audience.

I have played clubs so far into the "woods" that you would never believe anything was back there. Some of those clubs held 500 to 600 people and it would be packed. I have had to dress in kitchens, broom closets, standing on a chair over an overflowed toilet with no mirrors, no comforts at all after traveling over 400 miles to get there. Plus the club owners wanted you to sing all night, and even then they might refuse to pay you when you finish.

Because I never knew what would develop during the night, I started carrying a gun with me. Fights often broke out. I never knew when I'd have to stop the show and run for my life. True, there were some good club owners who tried to make it nice for us, but others just didn't care. Some of them did not respect you for no reason. The moment you got out of your car they started. I guess they were surprised you would actually come to their club. I was surprised, too, after I saw how they looked. But, I guess you would call me "lucky." I was in and out of the circuit. A few "pop" songs, like "Stand By Your Man" in 1971, took me to a lot of new areas in the business. I began to play mixed clubs—even the upper-class clubs, such as in Las Vegas. However, two years later, I was right back in the "circuit."

The circuit brings out the worst in an entertainer. First you develop the "I'm here to do my job, don't bother me" attitude. I began to use foul language the moment I got there. For good reason, too. At least I thought so.

First of all, promoters would get your promotional package in the mail and, if you were female and looked decent, he thought right away that he would spend the night with you. They took you completely for granted. Once I was booked in Chicago with three male entertainers on the show. I was the only female. This certain Chicago promoter sent my road manager back to the dressing room to get me, refusing to pay him.

"The promoter wants to see you", the manager said.

I was still wiping the sweat off my face after the performance. I got dressed and went down the hall to the promoter's office. He offered me a chair and a drink.

"No, thank you," I said. "I just came to pick up my money."

He walked around the desk, gathered me in his arms and tried to kiss me. I pushed him back, and he got angry. He threw my money all over the floor. There I was on my knees, picking it up. Can you see the mentality? Some promoters will send limousines to the airport to pick you up, take you to a hotel room where you would find their clothes already in the closet — and you had never met these guys before! The Chitlin' Circuit is rough.

Finally, in 1978 I got a manager who refused to deal with those kinds of clubs. He carried me in a totally opposite direction. He managed Mavis Staples and Ashford & Simpson. Disco was just beginning to be big. It had broken out everywhere, and my new manager geared me towards disco. That was a real big mistake. I was being labeled "disco." Disco is almost like the "Chitlin' Circuit" except I performed for whites, in mostly gay clubs. I was getting so well-known in the gay circuit that I was filling up those clubs every night.

I learned a lot during that period of my life. My heart reached out to the gays. I had so much compassion for them and I really loved them. I know their life-style was ungodly, yet I knew God still loved them. I used to see them bound and confused, taking all kinds of dope just to cope with their personal circumstances. I hate the demon that has them possessed. I now know they can be free, in the name of Jesus.

I used to talk to some of the gays I met. "I can't help it. I was born like this," some said.

"So was the man lame from his mother's womb. But, God healed him, and you can be free, too, only if you want to be. You've got to want it with all of your heart," I replied.

I have come to understand the Word of God and its principles. What we are dealing with in homosexuality is the transfer of a spirit. No doubt, when the person was very small, maybe as a baby in the crib, there was a person that held them, took care of them, or baby-sat them. A baby's spirit is wide open to receive anything. If the parents of that child had not dedicated the baby to the Lord and bound every unclean spirit from that child, the child is susceptible to any spirit including homosexuality. Hosea 4:6 says, "My people perished from the lack of knowledge." That is why we need to submit ourselves to a Bible believing church, so we can learn how to live Godly in this life.

I stayed in disco almost four years. I was in disco and "Chitlin' Circuit" clubs, as well as some "pop" shows. I also did the Midnight Special T.V. show with Lou Rawls and Johnny Mathis. I became a swinger. I was single and I was into women's lib. I believed in every right they said women should have and more. I believed in abortion. I had no reservations about anything. I was free to live my life any way that pleased me. I didn't have to answer to anyone. I made my own money, I could do my own thing. Oh, if I had only realized how wrong I was.

I had begun to date. It didn't matter who my dates were. This was my way of getting back at the world, but I was only hurting myself. I had no second thoughts about dating football players, basketball players, club owners, disc jockeys, heads of record companies, and famous entertainers. If I felt myself getting too serious, I would stop being available. I didn't want to ever again be serious about anyone. It really became a game to me, seeing who I could "get." The more famous they were, the more of a challenge they were, and I loved challenges. I was playing a dangerous game. I didn't mind dating other women's husbands. "They dated mine," I rationalized to appease my conscience.

This went on for a couple of years and I started getting sick just looking at myself. I felt rotten to the core, and I was. I began drinking more and more, to try and cover up my feelings. I just wanted to be loved. That's all I ever really wanted, yet I got everything but love. I had hurt so many people. I was mixed up and confused. When I was alone at night, I cried most of the time. I couldn't face some of the things I had done. I had a desire to be good again. I really wanted to, but I was so weak. The flesh is weak and that's why we need Jesus. When I'm weak, He becomes strong in my life.

I wish I had given Him my life before I met my next husband, because I know I wouldn't have gone through some of the things I did. Yet, God knows your breaking points and you have to go until you are broken. You have to come to the end of your will, where you can say, like Jesus, "Lord, not my will, but Thine be done."

Chapter 7

The Hunter Gets Captured By The Game

After I had gone through the swinging part of my life, I thought I could be good by getting married again. So I began to look for a husband. I wanted to stop all of the foolishness and settle down and raise my kids like a normal mother. That was on my mind when I was booked on a tour in California The promoter of that particular tour was very nice to me. He sat with me in my dressing room all night and kept me company. He ordered champagne and we toasted and just had a good time together in the dressing room. After the show, we found a nice quiet restaurant to have breakfast before he took me to the hotel. He never made sexual advances toward me. It was friendship and business all the way.

I began to like him. He was different. If I had only known how different. He told me things I wanted to hear about myself. He wouldn't allow me to put myself down. I really needed to hear that from somebody because by that time I had a poor self-image. I clung to his compliments with every fiber of my being. "Maybe I'm not so bad, after all," I thought.

Little by little he wiggled his way into my life. While the tour was going on, I had a birthday. I just casually mentioned it to him one night and he smiled. The night of my birthday, he invited me to a room in the hotel and, lo and behold, there was a big party. I had never had a birthday party in my life, and I was flattered. All of his friends were there, some of them wearing minks and diamonds. They looked like the "Superfly" movie characters. In another room he had soup bowls filled with cocaine and mountains of weed. I got scared, because if the cops came, man, I didn't want to go to jail. "Don't worry about it," he said, admitting that he knew.

But I still felt a little uneasy just being there. I only drank the champagne, then I went back to my room. I couldn't get that scene out of my head. If I had only listened to my heart—not my head, I would have avoided a lot of pain and problems that I was soon to face.

When the tour ended, we went back home. I was sort of relieved to be away from him because I had mixed feelings about him. There was a certain mystique about him—an attractive evilness that I couldn't understand.

One week later he came to Atlanta. He was downtown. I went to his hotel to see him and spent the night. That is when I became serious about him. After that night, things were really working in his favor, so he wanted to meet my kids. I took him by my house, and when he saw it he was just taken with the beauty of the place. I had a big, contemporary house with all new furniture, on two acres of land with a well-kept lawn. I was very happy with the place and proud that I had accomplished this all by myself.

But I wasn't happy otherwise. There was always an ache inside of me. I wanted something more to make my life complete. I kept thinking "I need a husband but I've already had two, and they didn't make my life any easier." Yet I never seemed to learn. We make the same stupid mistakes over and over without Jesus in our lives.

All of a sudden, this new man in my life was struck by love. Oh, he was so "in love" with me. He didn't ever want to leave me. I was "everything he's ever wanted in a woman." God "had sent me from Heaven just for him." Oh, I could go on and on.

"Hey," I told him, "I'm not ready for marriage yet so you better go back to California." I still had this nagging feeling saying, "Leave him alone — he's bad news."

But I let lust rule in his favor. Two weeks later he showed up at my house again. This time he brought his friend with him. He said they only came back to Atlanta to invest in some property. I really didn't want to see him but he kept calling and calling. He took me out to dinner. We laughed and had fun, and I ended up spending the night with him again. Then, he began to open up to me. Oh, he had a sad story to tell me about his childhood and his life. What an easy mark I was. I began to feel compassion for him. He came to my house and stayed for a few days. The days turned into weeks and he again asked me to marry him. I didn't want to get married — certainly not to him. I felt like, "This is just not the guy."

One morning, after he had been there a few weeks, he announced he had a weird dream. He knew about my religious background, so he used that. He said he dreamed about fire and water and God. God told him I was supposed to be his wife. God, he said, gave him a number to call. He called this number and it was the health department. The lady on the phone told him that I could get married in a day and told him where to go and everything. I laughed. That was the funniest thing I had ever heard! He didn't like my laughing.

"I'm going to fix you the best breakfast you've ever had," he said.

He went into the kitchen and he began to prepare my breakfast. I had already forgotten about the marriage thing and my thoughts were on something else when he came back with the tray.

"I'm not hungry," I told him. "I don't want this."

"It's okay."

So he ate some of the food and said, "Just drink your coffee."

After I drank the coffee, I had no will power. I can't tell you to this day what happened but I became a "yes" person. It was as if I was in a trance. I obeyed him. Everything he said, I obeyed. He even went to the closet and picked out my clothes. I said, "Oh, that's pretty." I was under mind control from that day on.

We went to the courthouse, got married, came home and told the kids. They did not like him at all. They dropped their heads and went in five different directions. They couldn't believe I could do something so stupid. They knew he was a phony from the first day they met him, but they thought I was lonely and needed company so they didn't say anything. They never dreamed I would marry the guy.

He began to tell me about all of the money he had. He was supposed to be a mortician, but he wasn't. He said he owned a funeral home in Oakland, California but he didn't. He never did. He said the IRS had all of his money tied up in a lien. That was a lie. I could have lived with him not having money but I couldn't live with the lies and violence. He became mean, so violent, not only to other people, but to me and my kids. He would threaten me when I mentioned divorce. He said he would kill my kids if I ever mentioned leaving him. I was so scared of him, I began to break out in hives and itch all over. I knew I had to get away from him, but how?

One night at an Army base club in Oklahoma, he was on stage as emcee. He completely took over my business. He even began to sing. He'd always wanted to be an entertainer, and he finally had access to somebody's stage. The audience began to heckle him. The commanding officer came back to the dressing room. "Miss Staton, when are you coming on? We are getting complaints. They want that guy off."

I walked out and beckoned him to cut it. He got mad, but finally called me on. The second show went the same way. After I left the stage and said good night to the audience, he was still up there clowning. People walked out on him. The officer came back to the dressing room again. "We have got to be out of here at a certain hour. We must close. Stop that guy."

So, I went back to the stage and told the musicians to stop playing, to just leave him up there by himself. They were glad to do it. They walked off.

He became livid. He stormed into the dressing room, jacked me up beside the door, and called me every name he could think of. He pulled a gun out of his briefcase and threatened to kill me and all of my musicians. "Nobody embarrasses me like that and gets away with it!" he shouted. "I'm going to kill them!"

I ran behind him begging him not to hurt anyone in the band. "I told them to do it," I screamed. "Don't blame them!"

But he wouldn't listen. He pulled the gun on them and dared them to load any equipment into the bus. He was going to leave them in Oklahoma. I spoke up for them. "Well, if you leave them, you'll leave me too."

He turned from them, pushed me against the car, and put the gun directly at my nose and threatened to kill me. I have never been so frightened in my life. Fans were coming by for autographs, but when they saw what was happening, they quickly turned around and left. That was one of the most frightening and embarrassing nights of my entire career. I have always been respected in the business because I carried myself with respect. What I did in my private life the public never knew. But when it came down to business, it was 100 percent business. This guy was ruining my reputation. He swore and acted like a raving maniac. You get in the car," he said. "I'm taking you back to the hotel."

On the way back to the hotel, he called me every curse word he could think of. I wanted to kill him. I know how a battered wife feels because I've been one. You can't explain the pain to anyone. It's a love-hate relationship. Sometimes you feel sorry for your husband and protective of him. My situation got totally out of hand that night. We were about two blocks away from the hotel, when he put me out of the car at 4 A.M.... Here I was in this Army town, and he told me to walk. He put me out of my own car! I cried and I shook all over.

As soon as he pushed me out and sped away a car of drunken soldiers pulled up. As I walked past a garage of another hotel, the soldiers said, "Hey, baby, you look like you need a man," and they got out of the car. "Oh, God," I said. "Not now, Lord. I can't take any more of this tonight." They tried to get me into their car.

As they attempted to force me in, a security guard came out of nowhere. As far as I was concerned, he may as well have been an angel. They got back into the car after the guard had warned them of the consequences. He asked me why I was out this time of night. I told him my husband and I just had a fight and he had put me out of the car. The guard just shook his head. "Where do you live," he asked.

I told him the name of the hotel where I was staying.

"I'll walk you to your hotel," he said and he saw me safely there.

After getting into my room, I sat there seriously thinking of how I could murder my husband, and get away with it. I knew I had to get away from him because I was so afraid of him. Fear is really something! It will cause you to stay or leave. He came back to the hotel close to daybreak as though nothing had happened. He just smiled and tried to apologize, as if it had been just a normal every-day occurrence. I can't begin to describe in words how much I hated that man. Satan was right there whispering in my ear saying since you can't divorce, put a contract out on him and have him killed! Satan will cause a situation, get you in trouble and then leave you alone to suffer the consequences.

We finally left Oklahoma. Everyone was silent all the way home. My husband was the only one who was jolly. Oh, he joked and laughed and tried to make friends, but nobody responded.

When we got back to Atlanta, the word quickly spread: "Don't go on the road with Candi Staton! Her husband is crazy!" So musicians would almost hang up on me when I called. It was really bad. Here is a man not bringing in any money and standing in my way of making money, too. Club owners heard about him. He would walk into a club after we had driven four or five hundred miles and demand the money almost before we unloaded. The club owner would get mad and say, "Man, pack up. I don't need this. I'll cancel the show."

You couldn't talk any sense into him. He acted possessed. Now that I know about demons and how they rule a person's life, I'm sure he was possessed. After the reports about him circulated, I couldn't buy a gig. Singing was my living, so bills came due. I could no longer meet my obligations because he had used a lot of my money. When he asked me for money I just gave it to him because I was so afraid of him. To keep down confusion, I gave him what he wanted. Warner Brothers heard that nobody would hire me, and they sent for us. They had heard how my husband had cursed out deejays and how, as a result, they were no longer playing my records. You don't talk badly to deejays. You highly respect those guys because they can influence record sales.

We went to California to meet with Warner Brothers. Twelve men met with us, including the chairman of the board, the president, and the vice-president. They brought up everything they had heard, and naturally we denied everything.

"If you want to stay on this label, Candi, you are going to have to get a manager. Do you object to that?" The executives said.

"No," I answered.

I knew if Warner dropped me, no other record company would pick me up, not under those circumstances. So my husband agreed also. We went home and Warner started looking for a manager. I was so disgusted with my husband, that I wanted to choke him. He was better after the meeting. He really tried to be good, but the Bible says that when you want to do good, evil is always present. Nobody can be good alone.

It takes the Holy Spirit living in us to make us good. Now whenever I said, "I'm going to divorce you," he would burst out and start crying, begging, "Please don't leave me!" I hated him, but I didn't know what to do. I felt deep down in my heart I would never get out of this marriage alive. I knew one of us was going to die. Only God could straighten out this mess. So, I did the only thing I hadn't done yet. I began to pray.

"God, please get me out of this one." Meanwhile, I had lost my house because of my financial situation. A seemingly endless pile of bills was due. We moved away from Atlanta to Reston, Virginia, in the Washington, D.C. area, near my brother. My brother hated my husband too. "Candi, where did you find this fool?" he would ask.

My whole family was disgusted with me. My husband was a pathological liar, and everybody knew it but me. I still tried to believe in him, but that's the way mind control works. Don't say that it could never happen to you, because if you don't have God in your life, you too are vulnerable to such Satanic powers. Bob Dylan sang a song, "You Gotta Serve Somebody," and that's absolutely true. That's why I love the Lord so much. I think about where He brought me from, even as filthy as I was. He still loved me. He was still looking out for me and protecting me.

After we had lived in Virginia for a year, I remember walking in the park by myself and praying. "God, if You only get me out of this, I will give You the rest of my life. Please, God, help me. You are the only one who can" and I really meant it. I began to feel a presence, like somebody was watching over me. I prayed this prayer every day, and all during the night.

One night I had a nightmare in which I saw this man running after me. I was worn out, gasping for breath. When I looked back at him, he had my husband's face. But he had a wicked smile and two horns growing out of his head. I was so frightened, I woke up in a cold sweat, and a voice said, "The only way you can get rid of him is to go home. . . ." I didn't realize what that meant. I thought, "I am at home." Then, the voice said, " where your mother is." I know now why I was told to go home because that was the closest thing to love I had. If I was surrounded by love, even if it was family love, it would weaken Satan's hold. Plus, I had a praying mother there.

My mother became ill the following week and I went to Alabama to check on her. While I was there, an old family friend stopped by to visit her. He got ready to leave.

"By the way, I have a choice piece of property I would like to sell. If you know anyone who needs some property, let them know," he said.

"I'm looking for property!" I said.

"Girl, I know you don't want to come back here and live," he replied.

"I've been thinking about it."

"Well, do you want to see it now?"

"Why not?" I quickly answered.

I got into his truck and, we went to the property site and walked the acreage.

"How much?" I asked.

He told me and I wrote a check on the spot. A deed was made later, and the land was mine. I called my husband.

"Guess what I just did! I just bought five acres of land!"

"That's great," he replied. "What are you going to do with it?"

"I'm going to build a house so I can be near my mother."

The last thing I figured he would ever want to do was live in the country, a pimp-type like him. But he agreed to it. God was definitely working. I found a contractor and started looking for plans suitable for my family. I found the perfect house. We went to the bank, and the president loaned us the money. They approved it in a matter of days. Just as fast, the contractor started to lay the foundation. I was so excited! While they were building the house, my mother became extremely ill. I returned to Alabama to put her in the hospital. I decided we might as well put our things in storage and move in with her so I could look after her.

In the meantime, I picked up a book by Norman Vincent Peale and began to read it often. In fact, I carried it in my purse. The book helped me a lot by encouraging me to pray all the time. My mother and I talked constantly about the Lord, too. That would just irk my husband. He would leave during those discussions.

"There's something evil about him," my mother would say, "you had better pray."

He couldn't really raise a fuss like he was used to doing so he was rather cool around my mother. I knew he was uncomfortable. His style was really cramped now. I could see an uneasiness developing in him. I knew it was only a matter of time before he would explode. He would try to pick an argument with me, but I wouldn't argue. I would leave the room and go to my mother's room. That made him angry.

One Saturday night I took the car and went over to a friends' house and stayed most of the day. When I came back he was fuming. He pouted all night. It was hot that particular night, and Clarence Junior, my 6-year-old, was uncomfortable. So I got up and made us a pallet on the floor, and fell asleep. I had another dream. I was reading Peale's book and he suggested if you wanted something real badly, you should write it down on a piece of paper and put it in your wallet, so you would have to look at it each time you went into your purse.

The note read, "There is nothing that will happen to me today that Jesus and I can't handle." In my dream I saw myself taking this out of my purse and reading it. I woke up sort of worried. Why did I dream a dream like that? What's going to happen today? Is my mother going to die? I've never thought the dream was intended for me.

After my husband woke up, he washed up, sat on the porch, then he called me. I went to see what he wanted.

"We've got to talk. Let's go to our house," he said.

When I got in the van, something spoke to me and said, "Don't go there to talk."

"I'm not going out of this yard," I said.

With that, he started to reveal his dislikes and frustrations. I sat and listened. Then something came over me. I can't explain it, but I wasn't afraid of him anymore.

"I've had it with you," I said, "and this time I mean it. Whatever you are going to do to me, do it now, cause I'm divorcing you."

"What?" he said. He jumped out of the car, stomped his feet and screamed, "Didn't I tell you never to say that to me again? I'll teach you!"

He ran into the house and got the gun. My cousins were outside, washing the car, and started screaming, "Run, Candi! He's got a gun!!" My first impulse was to run. I started up the van and he began shooting at the van. Then something inside me said, real loud, "STOP! HE CAN'T HARM YOU!"

My mother was out of bed, on the porch, screaming, "Please don't kill my baby! Oh Lord, don't let him kill my child!"

I turned the ignition off and he ran to my side and put the gun directly in my face. I began to laugh. I really was not scared. I was just relaxed. It was unreal. I looked at him.

"Go on! Shoot me! You want to shoot me, but you can't because God won't let you," I said.

He dropped the gun and opened the door of the van and began to beat me in my face but I miraculously didn't feel a thing. Ordinarily, I'm easy to bruise, but I didn't get one bruise.

"Now, do you feel better?" I said. "I'm going into the house, and I'm going to call the police. You can stay if you want to."

I got out of the van, and started for the house. He got into the van and drove away.

When I think of that incident, I shiver. But for the grace of God, I could be dead today. That gun had real bullets. That man was like a caged animal, surrounded by my family. He had nowhere to go. I can see now how God loved me even as a sinner. I had not given my life totally to Him, but I really wanted to. My intentions were good. But, by no means was I finished with my husband.

My husband finally left for good at my mother's request. I had a station wagon and a van. He took the van and loaded it with all of his clothes. I really didn't care what he took, just as long as he got away. He first went to Texas to live with some people he knew. He called me every few minutes, but I wouldn't talk to him. He would call and call and call until we would get so disgusted we left the phone off the hook. It was the only way we could rest.

My mother became sick again and we had to put her back into the hospital. I was at the hospital with her most of the time, so he started phoning. I refused to talk to him. Then he called a local undertaker and sent him to the hospital to get my mother. She wasn't dead! The undertaker entered the room.

"I've come to pick up the body."

"Shoo!" I said. "Be quiet!"

I rushed him out of the room and asked what was going on. He said a guy told him he was her son and had told him to go and get his mother's body.

"She's not dead!" I said angrily.

He apologized and left.

My husband was like the devil, he was crazy. Next, he sent my mother a weird flower, a kind of flower not ordinarily sent to a sick person. There was something about that flower that terrified my mother so I got rid of it. He kept calling, threatening me, saying he was going to kidnap my baby. I lived in constant fear.

Time came to close the deal on the house but I couldn't close without my husband's signature because his name was on the deed. I tried to get my lawyer to change it, but he could do nothing. My husband wouldn't sign anything. He threatened to sue me, and finally did, for $250,000 and a percentage of everything I would make in the future. He wanted to automatically get a percentage of any future record contracts or future concert dates for the rest of my life. I began to pray and ask God to please help me again.

My lawyer came up with a big, bright idea, "Go back to him." I felt sick to my stomach. I jumped up. "No way!"

"Sit down," he said, "and let me finish. I've got a plan. He can't sue you twice for the same thing in this court. I know the judge; if he ever throws this out it's out for good. Go back to your husband long enough to straighten this mess out, then you can walk out when you get ready."

"Let me think about it," I told my attorney.

I had a new manager who took over all of my business. My manager was also a lawyer. He hit the ceiling when I told him my plan, but when I explained why, he understood. Still, he was definitely not pleased. I phoned my husband. "I want to see you,"

He was in the city a matter of hours. That's when I discovered I could act. I should have gotten the Academy Award for my performance. I convinced him I wanted to try again. I was sick to my stomach through the whole experience. I'll never forget it. We canceled the divorce, he signed the papers for the house, the bank released the money to the contractor. Now here I was, back with this maniac again. What now, Lord? After I took him back, he got worse.

We prepared for a London tour and applied for visas and passports. I discovered his name was not what I knew it to be. He had a hard time getting a passport. He went and had his real name officially changed to the name I knew him by—the name I thought I already was! All the years I had been married to this fraud, I was married with the wrong name! Can you imagine waking up one day and finding out you've never been Mrs. X, but Mrs. Y instead?! We went on to London with the Stylistics.

That was the worst tour I can ever remember doing in my life. He cut up, he got drunk, got sick, talked loud. One night while in England, on the way from a gig, we stopped for food. He was drunk and he started an argument with a group of punk rockers.

Jewell Gospel Trio
Candi Staton (13), Naomi Harrison and Maggie Staton

Candi at Sweet 16

Marcus Williams, Terry Williams, Cassandra
Williams (being held), Marcel Williams, Candi Staton Williams

My Brothers and Sisters

Robert Earl Staton, Maggie Staton Peebles, Candi Staton and Joe Staton

Joe Frazier and Candi at Capital Records
party with D.J's and Promotion men. 1969

Candi Staton 1976
Picture plaigarized by Sugar Hill Records
(never did get any royalties from them)

On stage in Seattle, Washington - 1976

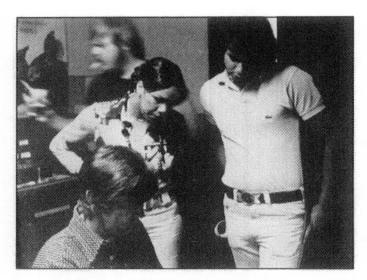

When I signed with Warner Brothers.
Rich Hall (seated) My Producer

Candi with Ashford and Simpson
at a Warner Brothers party.

Warner BrothersParty at Studio 54 in New York, NY
Stephanie Mills, Candi Staton and Diana Ross

Candi Staton with B.B.King - 1973

The Commodores & ME!

Candi Staton-Sussewell and Roy Clarke
Richard Roberts Live Show - 1989

Grammy Awards - 1984
Andre Crouch, Candi Staton and Sandra Crouch

Candi and Jim Bakker pose for picture after concert
in Federal Prison, Jesup Georgia. January 1994

Candi Staton-Sussewell with Chuck Swindoll
at SuperBowl Chapel XXII - San Diego, CA

Steven Curtis Chapman, Michael Ward and
Myself at Melody Green's Artist Retreat - 1990

Demond Wilson (former star of Sanford and Son)
w/Candi Staton-Sussewell Fort Lauderdale, FL - 1985

Dr. Myles Munroe and Candi
Women's Aglow Fellowship in Jamaica - 1991

Candi with best friend Debbie Bartlett of Nassau, Bahamas
on vacation in Waikiki Beach, Honolulu

TBN Praise-A-Thon

Paul and Jan Crouch, Steve Brock, The Tripp Family, The Rambos and Nancy Harmon

My first Holy Land Tour after I was saved - 1986 Israel

All five of my children and my Son-in-Law Calvin Hightower
(Left to Right) Marcus, Marcel, Cassandra, Calvin, Terry and Clarence

John & Candi Sussewell

The whole band, including my manager, got up and eased out and left him in there ranting and raving. When he finally got away, he got on the bus and began pulling my hair, in front of my band, my manager, and all the Stylistics, and dared anyone to get up. He was sickening! I kept saying to myself, "I can't wait until this tour is over." Then I braced myself and thought, "Just be cool, Candi."

He woke up every morning and ordered the most expensive champagne. I brought home absolutely no money. One night, after the show, he wanted to have sex. I couldn't stand him, so I refused. When I started to leave the room, he grabbed me, threw me on the bed, and began to tear off my clothes. I fought him, but I couldn't handle him. He was too strong and he raped me. I laid on the bed after he left, and cried and cried and cried. I felt so dirty! I laid there for a long time just sobbing. I felt numb, used, and sick. I hated myself and I hated him. The sobs kept coming, deep, racking sobs.

"I hate him!" I cried. "Oh God, I hate him! God, did you make him, too? Or did he come straight from the pits of hell? I know I'm not supposed to hate, but I can't help it!"

I got a good feeling every time I pictured him dead. I wanted him dead. Then I would say, "God, forgive me for that thought." I just wanted out. That was all, just out. The tour finally ended, and we came back home. Now, I thought, it's time to make the final move.

It worked out so perfect, it was as if it was planned. My girlfriend just happened to drive up from Atlanta to see me. As soon as we got back he and I were arguing furiously. She suggested I go home with her to Atlanta to stay a few days. I sent my kids over to my mother's house because I didn't want them staying with my husband. I didn't trust him.

As soon as I got to Atlanta, the calling from my husband started again—every 10 minutes. We had to take the phone off the hook. Then my girlfriend got fed up with the whole mess. She started acting strange, as though she didn't want me there. She made strange remarks and started to act as if I wanted her boyfriend.

I got the message and left the next morning. I arrived home that evening to find my husband had had a fit. Windows had been broken out of the house. The closet doors had been torn down. The phone had been thrown against the wall several times. "What happened?" I asked, stunned.

He responded with a tale about the mafia having been there and threatening him because he was letting this marriage fall apart. He wasn't supposed to do that, he said, and I was the cause of it.

Before an argument could begin, my sister from Nashville drove up unexpectedly. "Saved by the bell!" I thought. It was perfect timing. "Let's go over to Mama's house," I said to her.

As soon as we got into the car, I started to explain what was happening. "Let's go and get your money out of the account," she suggested, "and go to Nashville and you can get an apartment. Let him stay in the house, since he refuses to leave by himself."

I went back to the house (my clothes were already packed from Atlanta) and got my kids' clothes together, and told him we were going to Nashville for a few days to sort things out. He was angry, but didn't say much. I went to Nashville and got an apartment. The next day I rented furniture, bought bedclothes, and started living there. I rented a van after two weeks and went back to the house to get some more things.

My husband went into hysterics. He screamed, "What am I going to do? You can't leave me like this!"

He even called the police on me and lied, saying I was taking all of his things. They came and demanded I put everything back except my clothes. My stepfather took one of the officers around to the back of the house to explained the real situation. They came back into the house and apologized to me, and told me to take what I wanted to take. My husband looked puzzled, but he remained calm. I stayed in Nashville for two months. Meanwhile, the electricity and the telephone were disconnected at the house and he had no money to even buy food. He was going all over the community, I was told, sitting around until someone offered him dinner. He got up one morning and asked my neighbor if he would take him to the airport. He wrote Delta a bad check and went back to California.

I got a divorce by default because he didn't show up for court. I have seen him twice since, once in a disco in Chicago, and once in Philadelphia. He cornered me in Philadelphia and threatened me again. After that, I've never seen him again. But off and on, he managed to get my phone number, disguise his voice and call. I would recognize his voice every time. It was three years before he stopped calling, and I haven't heard from him since.

Chapter 8

Why Won't The Pain Go Away?

Single again. I was so lonely, yet I was afraid to get involved with anyone. I figured if I got involved with someone, he might kill me. So I made up my mind to be a satisfied single. I dated, I would have one-night stands, but no permanent relationships. I was frightened. Men frightened me and I trusted no one.

I threw myself into my work. I neglected my kids for my work while I stayed in New York for three straight months. I didn't worry about them, they were in the country and I figured there was nothing they could get into. I knew the children needed me, but I was selfish. I tried to find happiness by becoming a superstar. I should have been obsessed with becoming a supermom, but my priorities were mixed up. The devil will always mix up your priorities. I would look at guys, and every guy's face would soon be my ex-husband's. So I said, "I'll never marry again." I had had enough of abuse. This went on for three years.

In that time, my manager and I became close friends and drinking buddies. He was a very successful lawyer. Boy, did we drink in style! I had never before gotten blasted at a fine restaurant in Beverly Hills on the best alcohol in the place. But when I did, I found out a rich drunk feels just like a poor drunk. A drunk is a drunk. We went out to dinner together almost every night. When we weren't going out to dinner in limousines and Rolls Royces, we were going to his apartment getting drunk. He was an alcoholic, too. I had found my drinking partner. Boy, was I having fun, I was going down smiling! I desired to be with him so I could drink. When I thought of him, I thought of alcohol. I got to a point where I was really getting hooked. I gained weight. I didn't eat sometimes for two days, but I still gained weight. My hands started to swell, my feet felt puffy all the time. I was bloated. My skin sometimes looked paper thin. I began to need to drink. I desired it. It became my husband, my lover, my kids, my comforter, my friend, my everything, my god. I worshipped alcohol.

Nobody really knew how bad off I was. I would drink all day and not eat anything. I used to see the wall move. I started seeing snake-like images on the floor, sometimes on my bed, I saw little insects that weren't there. I had lapses of memory. I was incoherent. I lost touch with the world and I barely functioned. I would fall asleep, then wake up abruptly and sit up in the bed shaking. Yet I wanted more and more. My kidneys began to hurt and I had pus in them. The doctor told me if I wanted to keep my kidneys I had better stop drinking. I thought about what he said, until I needed another drink.

"Forget him. He can't tell me what to do," I said reaching for a bottle. I would have my antibiotics in one hand and my scotch in another. It got to a point where I wasn't very pleasant if I wasn't drinking. I had to have a drink to be sociable. Warner Brothers held a press party for me, and I would hit the bar before the party, knowing that alcohol was available. I wanted to be halfway there prior to the party so it didn't seem like I was drinking too much during it. I gulped down liquor until I got to the level of high I wanted, then I could coast all night, just sipping. I was so bound! I wanted to be free of this but I didn't know how (read Proverbs 23:29-35).

My two oldest sons were worried. They would take my bottles and hide them from me. In a furious frenzy, I would talk to them so badly that they would give them back to me. "Mom, we are worried about you. Please don't drink so much," they said.

"Shut up!" I would snap back. "I know what I'm doing."

I continued to drink in an almost constant state of pain in my kidneys and my urinary tract.

One night I started weeping. I was so unhappy, I couldn't stop. You can have the world and the devil still won't let you be happy. Looking back now I can see I had it all. I had five healthy kids, a good career with the world's greatest record company, a beautiful home, plenty of money, and there I was trying to drink myself to death. Isn't the devil the pits? I couldn't find happiness. Something was always missing. Now I know what that something was. It was Jesus. You can have it all but if you don't have Jesus, you have nothing. It took me a long time to find that out.

I'm so glad Jesus doesn't give up on us. He's still patient and forgiving, even though we don't deserve Him. I can't imagine what would have happened to me if God had said, "Well, I've given her a chance, and each time she blew it. Now, I'm through." That's what we say about each other. I just pray that I'll have the love and the mercy for someone else as He has for me.

That's why I love sinners so much. I want to gather them in my arms and love them because that's what Jesus did for me. He loved me and died for me while I was yet a sinner, protecting me by His tender mercy. Oh, how God could have judged me for being a rotten mother, a drunk, everything I was involved with was so wrong. Yet, He still loved me.

Oh, praise God, for His mercy endures forever. I am reminded of the prostitute in the Bible. The people interrupted Jesus' teaching to bring him a woman taken by adultery. The men wanted her stoned but Jesus stooped down and began to write something on the ground.

"You who are without sin cast the first stone," he said.

When He stood up and looked around, everybody was gone. He looked at the woman. "Where are your accusers?"

"I have no one Lord," she said.

"Neither do I condemn you, go and sin no more," he said.

That is the kind of God I serve, a loving merciful God!

Chapter 9

Still Looking For Love

When I began working on my twelfth album, I had been divorced for three years. This particular album, "I'm Looking for Love", followed the "Chance" album during which the Lord had spoken to me and told me that my career was over. We had a lot of difficulty finishing the project. Everything went wrong. We canned several songs and cut new ones to replace them. I began to think I would never finish the album, so did Warner Brothers and Jimmy Simpson, who co-produced with me. Jimmy took it upon himself to cut three more sides after I returned to my home in Alabama. He then called me back to Sigma Sound in New York to put vocals on those new tracks. It was there that I met John Sussewell. He came to do some overdubbing. John had a lot of experience as a drummer with many secular artists. Little did I know this man was about to become a permanent part of my life.

Though I had heard of John, my opinion of him was that he was just another run-of-the-mill New York musician. Boy, was I wrong. This man was not only talented, but well educated. "What is a smart guy like you doing in a place like this?" I thought.

The hours we spent in the studio seemed as dedicated toward my getting to know him as they were for me to put vocals on the new tracks my producer had cut. I found myself growing more and more interested as he shared his growing up experiences with me.

John was a freshman at Brooklyn Technical High School, when President Kennedy started a talent search program for some of the nation's brightest black boys and girls to attend private college prep schools around the country. John's mother, a guidance counselor for the New York City school system, was one of the local contact persons to help identify these young people.

Students at Brooklyn Tech had to take a qualifying exam in order to enter the school. The one year John attended there, he had honor grades. Therefore, as a minority student, he was in a good position to be selected to receive a federally funded scholarship. Out of the various students in private schools in New England, John was admitted to the sophomore class at Milton Academy in Milton, Massachusetts.

Milton Academy was founded in 1798 and had among its alumni the Kennedy's, the Morgans and many other well known individuals from American society. John was the first black admitted to the institution and he graduated with honors from this school.

Now you have to know that this was just not any school. One of John's classmates was Steve Bogart, the son of Humphrey Bogart and Lauren Becall. Joe Kennedy, son of the late Senator Robert Kennedy was also a student at the school and lived in the same dormitory as John. While there, John was appointed to be Joe's math tutor and worked very closely with him. John remembers vividly being thanked personally by Senator Kennedy for helping his son.

I began to see why I was so interested in John during our first meetings over dinner and during walks in New York City. He really surprised me when he started talking about his love of sports. Sam Jones of the Boston Celtics awarded John and four other New England private school basketball players for athletic achievements in their league. John's love of basketball seemed to have been inherited not only from the streets of New York but from his cousin who was Chuck Cooper, the first black man to play professional ball for the Boston Celtics.

But that wasn't all. John told me of his experiences with another school mate. The recording artist James Taylor attended Milton while John was there and had a tremendous influence upon the artistic climate of the school. John also found his musical outlet. Music was a very strong and visible activity for John at Milton with the formation of a dance band and singing group that stayed together through college.

John's drumming began before entering Milton. Morris Goldenburg, the late head of the percussion department at Julliard Conservatory of Music personally instructed him. They lived in his neighborhood of Bayside, Queens, New York. While playing in the concert band at Brooklyn Tech, John was selected from among New York City's young percussionists to play a park concert with the famed Goldman Band.

All of these experiences and achievements led up to John being admitted to Harvard University, Class of 1971, but not before Milton would honor him during graduation with several awards noting his outstanding influence in the field of music, his spirit of cooperation with fellow students who respected him and his self-sacrifice in the life of the School.

On the other hand, Harvard was a different experience for John. It was as less intimate. Where Milton was like a family, Harvard was like a small city. Where John's graduating class at Milton had only 54 students, John entered Harvard with 1024 other men and women. Milton helped to bridge John's emptiness coming from a broken home where his father deserted his mother. It seemed that Cambridge, Massachusetts would no longer provide the close support of friends and activities.

John shared with me one incident of racial prejudice while playing as second string goalie for the Freshman soccer team at Harvard – a team that was undefeated in its season. During a game where Harvard was winning by four goals in the final quarter, instead of putting him in to get some play, the coach bypassed him and chose a less talented player. John was unscored on during his senior year as a goalie for the Milton Academy team. He was used to getting play in soccer, basketball (Captain & MVP '67) and track (MVP '67 & a 120 yard hurdles record retired in 1982 when Milton changed over to the metric system).

When he approached the coach after the game to ask why he wasn't played, the response was less than what it should have been and it was evident that the man had a problem. There were no other blacks on the team except John. Before going on to be the national champs that year, John quit the squad. This was just one of many such incidents where John had a rude awakening about the state of the world outside of the protected Miltonian environment.

In spite of completing four years at Harvard, John told me that he was unable to make the proper adjustment to the life-style and more personal freedoms. By his junior year, he was involved in drugs which made his academic pursuits in electrical engineering and pre-medicine more difficult. His extra-curricular activities in music became a safety net and escape from his own inner conflicts and those of the nation's struggle with civil rights and the war in Vietnam.

A year off from Harvard to play with the horn band from the old Buddy Miles Express was a year that would steer John away from a career in medicine to one in the fame and glamour of the professional music industry. One of his classmates and fellow musicians who was enrolled at Radcliffe before the two colleges merged under the one name of Harvard is the now famous country/blues artist, Bonnie Raitt. The opportunity to work with other talented musicians and singers in the Cambridge and Boston communities began to overpower John's studies in the sciences. When the guitar player from his band was picked up by the then touring Staple Singers, John saw the strong possibility of him also succeeding as a drummer with named groups.

This was, in fact, the case. After finishing four years at Harvard, John was more interested in his music than anything else. This was to pan out for him. John came back to New York where relationships with several well known artists and groups began to develop and expose him to the 'scene.' Among the scene were Billy Cobham, Daryl Hall & John Oats, Mike Zagar & Ten Wheel Drive. Less than a year later the critically acclaimed Donny Hathway hired John to go on the road with him for the syndicated Newport Jazz Festival tours.

With Donny, John went from previous small club dates to play-ing in coliseums and concert halls across the nation and around the world before thousands: Carnegie and Avery Fisher Halls (NYC), Hampton Rhodes Coliseum (Hampton, VA), Riverfront Stadium (Cincinnati, OH) and many other venues both large and small in the U.S., Canada, England and Europe. He backed up with such artists as Bill Withers, Stevie Wonder, Esther Phillips, Freddie Hubbard, The Average White Band, Kokomo, Joe Cocker, Steve Winwood, Bette Midler, Ashford & Simpson, and Diana Ross.

Unfortunately, cocaine use had a growing influence in his life. As talented and as in demand as he was, his reputation began to decline.

You see, the music industry is big, but it's a small world in terms of gossip. People had been talking about John, saying he was losing his mind. The word had gotten around that he was a good drum-mer, very talented, yet something was happening to his life that he couldn't handle. So, when I started to ask for him, my co-producer said, "You don't want him. John's got a problem." But I said, "Yes I do," because he had been on Diana's album, "The Boss". I loved the disco, uptempo beat he had on that album. It was so consistent. I wanted that on my album because Disco was hitting pretty hard at the time. We went through the whole album without him, using other drummers. Sometimes we'd go in and record the same song twice or even three times, because we couldn't get exactly what we were looking for. After we had worked on this album for about three months, they finally called John Sussewell. Right away we got everything we wanted. It just clicked.

When I first saw John, I was definitely not impressed. He looked like anything off the street. He was unkempt, disheveled, with a long afro, matted together. He had on a turtleneck sweater, worn pants, and some cheap-looking shoes. I'm saying to myself, "This man is on all those albums; why in the world does he let himself go like this? Is that the best he can do?" I wondered. Yet, I was drawn to him. Shortly after we were first introduced, I walked over and started a conversation with him. I complemented him on his work on Diana Ross's album. He acted rather shy and withdrawn, but I continued to speak to him, asking questions, because I had heard all the rumors and I was curious about him. In spite of his shyness and the rumors about him I discovered during our conversations he was the most intelligent man I had ever met. Needless to say, I was confused, but very curious. I wanted to know more about this John Sussewell. John was very skinny — about six-foot-one, but only about 135 pounds — and I knew he had a problem. I didn't know what it was. I've always looked at a person beyond what they can do. I look at a person as a person, a human being, and I want to help if I can.

At one of the recording sessions, I went over to the keyboards to watch him play. He played well — good classical music. "Ummm," I said to myself, "so he plays piano, too." I was curious as to what made him tick. After the session, I invited him to go to the Sheraton to the 5:00 o'clock happy hour and have a drink. We went down there and started drinking and eating popcorn. We had time to get familiar with each other, but he never did tell me anything to reveal the real problem in his life.

JOHN SPEAKS: What really got me about having that opportunity with Candi was that, here was someone who was well-respected in the music industry, a star, and this 'star' showed more interest in me as a person than anyone I had ever worked for before. Candi and I just sat and talked. I never really told her about all of my problems. I buried most of them inside. All I really exposed to Candi was, 'I just went through a heavy divorce,' and 'I lost my baby girl in the process' . . . 'She's so sweet '. . .'My wife left me. . . .' and things like that. That divorce had been in 1978, and my little girl wasn't even a year old. When I exposed that, Candi felt that she was really inside of me. But there was so much more that I was hiding, things that she would find out later in our relationship.

CANDI SPEAKS: I had received invitation to Cheryl Lynn's birthday party. I invited John to go with me. Stars like Debbie Allen and Roberta Flack — famous musicians and producers — would be there. Warner Brothers sponsored it, and it was a party that John could have never gotten into on his own. When I asked him to be my escort, his eyes sparked up.

"Lord," I said to myself in a mock prayer, "let him go home and get dressed!"

"I've got to go home and change," he said, right on cue.

"You bet you do!" I thought to myself.

He left, and a while later came back, looking quite nice. He still needed a haircut, but I could deal with that. We had a good time, laughing a lot that night. The people in the business were very surprised to see him there, because usually John would do his job and go his own way. He was known as one of the best drummers in the business, yet he didn't flaunt it like some did. He definitely didn't have an ego trip going like many musicians. He was very low key, and I admired that about him.

We ended up spending the weekend together. In those three days, I became very fond of John. When I left on Monday evening, I really hated to leave him. But, I was three years out of my last marriage, pretty settled in my ways and not looking for a serious relationship or marriage. I was satisfied without marriage. Once you get through the first year after divorce, you're okay. I was running about, having a good time, but I was lonely. When you're a star, everybody thinks you're well. You have everybody around you, but stars are the loneliest people in the world. Everyone thinks, "I can't get close to that person, because she probably has people waiting on her hand and foot. She's probably got lots of boyfriends . . . I wish I was in her shoes."

Actually, after all the camera flashing goes off and you close that door and go into your room, you're one of the loneliest people in the world! You want somebody to talk to, but you can't talk to anyone! That's why drugs are such a common denominator in the industry. When the conversation hits a lull, there's cocaine, or alcohol, or marijuana. When all of that was gone, and the "friends" leave, there's still nothing but loneliness and that is where I was. John was a talkable person, and he enjoyed talking. I even loved his laugh! We just hit it off. I looked at him as being a friend, somebody in the business to talk to. That's as far as it was going. I had no plans for John Sussewell after I left New York. That had been my life for years, love 'em and leave 'em. I was a liberated woman.

I was home only about a week or two when I started to get lonesome again. John had been such good company! And here I was in this big house, alone. I had nothing to do for the next two weeks, my album was finished. So, I called John. It happened that I called him right in the middle of an argument he was having with his mother. I didn't know about that then, but I would find out later. His mother was on the verge of telling him to get out and start doing something with his life. John finally came to the telephone. "I miss you," he said.

"I miss you, too," I told him. "I want to see you. Can you come down?"

"I would love to, but I don't have the money right now."

"No problem. I'll send you a prepaid ticket."

He jumped at that idea. So I sent the ticket, and the next day he was there. As we got his luggage at the airport, I said to myself, "My! he sure brought a lot of clothes!" He had packed everything that belonged to him and brought it with him! "You'd think he's coming to stay!" I thought, amazed at the scene. "I told him a weekend!" But I just acted as though everything was "cool". We climbed into my station wagon and started up to my house in the country. It was a long drive, and he got acquainted with my sons on the way. Marcel, my oldest, was always a little reluctant to get too friendly with anyone I chose to date, because of my three ex-husbands. But, interestingly enough, he took to John. He really liked him. I was so pleased to have John there with me. Everything fit perfectly. I began to really care for him, not as just another guy, but for something real. I fell in love. I really didn't want this, because I was a few years older than he was and I kept reasoning, "When I get this age, he'll be that age. . . ." I would say to myself. "I can't let this go any farther." When he had been there three weeks, I took a walk by myself and came to the conclusion that this had to stop. Playtime was over. I came into the house after the walk. "I must talk to you. We've had our fun, but now it's time for us to go our separate ways."

He looked at me so sadly and said, "Candi, I love you. I just can't walk out like this. I don't ever want to leave you."

"But think of our age difference, John."

"I have. I don't care about age. I love you, and I want to be with you."

I told him we could see each other occasionally, but I didn't need a permanent relationship right now. We cried together and discussed it further and decided to try a little longer to see what happened. I probably would have ran from him if I had known his problem ran any deeper than his divorce. I didn't need his problems in my life! Even then, I knew the Lord was in our lives. He meant for us to be together. I believe that everything that happens does so for a reason. This was the way that the Lord had for saving John from death. If I had not come into his life right then, I don't know if John would be alive today and he agrees.

Chapter 10

Life's Revolving Doors

The time in the country had done John well—nothing but cows and chickens, far away from the big cities where he seemed to have so much trouble. He wanted so badly to stay. Within a few weeks, it was time to put a band together for touring. We began to look for musicians, rehearsing every day for several weeks until the band was tight and they sounded good. He asked to work for me and the band, so I hired him. Soon, with the money he earned, John was into new clothes and looking great.

Before John came in the picture, my manager, agent and I had taken care of the business. I encouraged John into another phase of the business which he was not familiar with, such as talking to with promoters and agents. He had never done that before. After two weeks John handled the phones like a professional, booking dates, calling offices, and talking to management. He was doing it all.

We didn't have a hit record off the "Lookin' for Love" album. We got airplay, but no big hits. We got just enough airplay to continue to work, but the records barely made it to the national Top Forty charts. They were what people in the industry call "turntable hits," which doesn't translate to sales. I fired my manager after that, and I left Warner Brothers. That increased the money we could keep by 20 percent.

I started trusting John. He didn't break that trust, either . . . that is, until we got back to New York. I didn't know how major John's problems were until that trip. And even then, I refused to accept how really bad it was. When you love someone, you believe lies. The Word of God says, "Love covers a multitude of sins" (1 Peter 4:8). And that is what happened.

Our first engagement was right back in New York City, where we had been four months before. After a three-day club date, we paid the band and put them on the road for the next date. John and I were to fly home. Warner Brothers wanted me to do some promotion while I was in New York. So one morning they sent a limo to pick me up and take me to record stores to sign autographs. When I came back to the hotel, John was gone. I laid on the bed and watched TV, thinking he would return soon. He didn't come back. Worried, I called his mother, thinking that maybe he was there, but she had not seen him either. Suddenly she began to cry. "He probably won't be back tonight," she sobbed. "Oh child, I've got to tell you. My son is hopeless. I thought he was over it, but he's not."

I still couldn't understand what she meant, so I started to ask questions. "Explain something to me, what does he do that I don't know about?"

"You don't know?"

Know what?

"I thought you knew," she began. "John is not well. He hasn't been for a long time." Then she started to cry even more. "He's addicted to cocaine."

I had some experiences with cocaine myself and I knew what effect it had on me, absolutely none. So I dismissed her evaluation.

"You can't get addicted to cocaine," I told her, sure of myself. "Anyone can tell you that."

"Yes you can, and John is," she answered right back. "Did John have any money when you last saw him?"

"Yes," I responded. "He has the whole payroll."

"Oh no! You didn't let him have your money, did you?"

"Y-Yes," I said with some hesitation.

We put a large sum of money in the safety deposit box downstairs in the hotel and John had the key. When I hung up the phone, I started walking the floor. I paced all night. I knew that John was scheduled to play the next morning with some jazz group that had found out he was in New York. I waited for him to come in, only dozing for a few moments the entire night. About 9:30 a.m. I heard the key turn in the door. In walked John. He looked awful, like something dead. I couldn't believe this was the John Sussewell I had fallen in love with.

"Where is my money?" I asked angrily.

"I got robbed."

What? Oh my God, no! All the money I worked for all week was gone. Marion Brown, John's mother had already warned me. I began to weep. He cried as well.

"Help me! Please Candi, you've got to help me! Don't throw me away! You can't throw me away! If you do, I'll die! I'll kill myself! I can't go on like this."

I cried, not for him, but for myself. I couldn't believe I'd done it again. God, what was wrong with me? Why couldn't I ever find a good man? How did I ever get involved with this? John's mother came over that evening and gave me some money. John and I already had our plane tickets, but I didn't want him to go back with me.

I said to him, "I'm not going through another hardship with a man or because of a man. Now, I think you should stay here in New York. It's your home, you know. I'll send your things to you."

"I'm not leaving you," he insisted. "I'm going to Birmingham with you. If I stay here, I'll die. Candi, you don't understand."

What does he mean? I thought to myself. I felt strange about this whole situation. I somehow knew this thing was a lot deeper than I could ever realize, but I still didn't know what was actually going on. After my anger subsided somewhat and he freshened up and became himself again, I yielded a bit. We left and went to Birmingham together. But the next morning I was still angry. Deep inside I kept thinking about the money he had lost. Other dates came up, however, and we gradually made the money back. Things appeared to be much better. Meanwhile, we would talk, but he never would allow us to talk about that. So it appeared we had weathered it all, and I thought it was over. I kept thinking his mother must be mistaken about him. John wasn't sick, I reasoned. Love is blind! The next thing I knew, John wanted to get married.

"I can't marry you!" I retorted.

But John was very persuasive, and I did love him. So after two months of him asking me, we decided to get married on December 24, 1980. We had a Christmas Eve concert engagement in Texarkana, Texas and the promoter found a minister there to marry us. We already had our license and blood tests. A Pentecostal minister and his bishop came to our hotel room and married us there. We went downstairs to the bar and ordered champagne, then went to the club to do the gig. My son, Clarence, was John's best man. Clarence, Jr. was nine years old. The show we did that night was the worst show I can ever remember, except perhaps my very first! Some ladies sat at the front table and heckled us during the entire show: "That music is too loud. Turn it down!" They were drunk, celebrating Christmas.

We finally loaded up and went back to the hotel. I was very happy in spite of everything. I had a good feeling about our marriage.

In the next few months, we continued to do concert engagements and everything was fine. John and I were getting along wonder- fully. I was happy... until we had a week stint at the Village Gate in New York. I didn't think too much about going to the city, though I did remember the last time, when I lost my money. I was confi- dent— that would never happen again. We weren't there a day before John disappeared. We were shopping, and I was looking at some blue jeans.

"I'll be right back," he said to me. "I've got to get some drum- sticks."

I didn't see him again until two days later.

Thank God my son, Marcus, could play drums extremely well, or I would have been "up the creek." My two oldest sons traveled with us. My oldest played bass, and my next-oldest played drums and percussion. So, when John was on drums, the usual setup was Marcus played percussion. But on these two nights, Marcus took

John's place, so nobody really knew John wasn't there, except the band. He also had the keys to our van, and it took six cabs to get us around. At least this time John only had maybe $200.00 of our traveling money... So we did the gigs without him. Nobody except the band knew anything was wrong. The place stayed packed out every night.

During that time, John's mother came by and explained some more about his "problem." I realized it only showed up when we went to New York. When John came back this time, he acted as though nothing had happened. I was puzzled. I wanted to know where he went, what he did. I accused him of having a girlfriend in New York he had never given up. "We are married now," I told him. "We are not supposed to keep secrets from each other. If you're not with a woman, please show me what you do when you stay away for days."

"You want to see what I do?" he asked sarcastically.

"Yes," I answered just as quickly. "I don't want you to go away. Feel free to do whatever you do – in this hotel with me. . . Just pretend I'm not here."

"Give me $300.00," he said. "I'll show you."

"I'll give you $150.00," I said, compromising.

He took the money and left.

He returned to the room with some pornography books and cocaine which he had just bought. I felt the presence of evil come in with him. Satan is so real!

Let me say that I never believed in evil spirits before this encounter. I believed in God because my mother taught me to, but not the devil! I believed the devil looked like the devil on the Devil's Lye can – two red horns and a tail. And that's one of the reasons why people are so defeated. Hosea 4:6 says, "My people are destroyed for lack of knowledge: because thou hast rejected knowledge, I will also reject thee..."

I got up and reached over the drawer in the dresser for the Gideon Bible. I put it into my pillow and held on to the pillow for dear life. I kept praying, "Protect me Lord." This went on for hours

— until I couldn't take it any more. Finally, I said, "Okay. Enough. I've seen enough! Stop it now!" But he couldn't. He had been taken over by an unseen force. His mind was completely out of control. He must obey Satan now.

Satan comes in all forms. He will use the body of anyone who will allow him. Satan, a spirit, was cast out of heaven. But for him to operate in the physical world, he needs a physical body. John yielded his body to the devil's power because he had no knowledge of God. Although, at an early age of nine, he walked down the aisle of a church for water baptism and admission into church, he was only submitting to a form of godliness and not its power. He was never taught that his enemy was the devil.

The fantasies he was experiencing was a perversion of the brilliant mind that God had given to him. Satan had corrupted it. Whatever God gives you for His glory, satan will want to take it and pervert it, if you yield to him. My husband is very smart and educated. In fact this was one of the positive attributes that attracted me to him. I knew he was nobody's fool, but satan deceived and stole this wonderful gift from him until he had him under his clutches. This kind of hold can only be broken by the power that is in Blood of Jesus.

Finally John left. I didn't see him again until the next morning. I still couldn't believe what I had witnessed the day before. Now I understood, what his mother and all those other people had been trying to tell me. He did indeed have a problem. Now that I knew what he did when he was away, I was concerned about his mind. I feared that he was on his way to destruction. Nobody could continue to do this without eventually reaping its devastating effects.

JOHN SPEAKS: I was **bound** by cocaine **and the lusts of the flesh.** I was also bound by the false expectation that these kinds of activities would help to replace the hurt, disappointment and rejection that I had experienced from time to time in my life.

The cocaine would feed that. That problem had been five years in the making. It wasn't always like that. I used to be able to use cocaine socially, but after a while it was a catalyst for a Dr. Jekyll and Mr. Hyde type of personality. When I took the money out of the safe that time, I just didn't care if it hurt Candi. At first I took a couple of hundred dollars — and I got two grams of cocaine with it. We left each other about 11:00 that day. Candi had left to do the store appearances, and I was supposed to see the band out of New York City. So by the time that eight hours was up, I realized that I was wired. I had another gram, or something like that, but I knew I wanted more. So I went back to that safe deposit box. It was the spirit behind the drug that was driving me. It wasn't me. In my heart I knew I was hurting Candi, but my mind justified it. I was deluded. I never did anything out of character when I wasn't under the influence of cocaine.

You think you can get a little of it, and then you make the mistake of taking a little money to get it. 'Oh, let me go buy about $50.00's worth, or $100.00,' I'd say. One gram of cocaine was good for eight hours for me, just by myself. I'd never share it. Just one gram of cocaine was like an eight-hour constant . . . the rush was over in about two minutes; so I could do that for about eight hours without running out. By the time I'd had an eight-hour high, I would be wired. My only drive then was to get more money.

It got to the point, even in that delusion, that I started literally selling my soul to Satan, who is very real! He bought it! He bought me! But you see, Satan is a liar. Even then he lied to me, every time I thought I would accomplish my goal, the prospect would disappear into thin air just like the drug. Sometimes the prospect would be the success in getting more without the money; jiving the dealer who trusted my music industry status more than he did my obvious condition at the time. Other times the prospect would be to success-fully hide this experience from those who could quickly bring it to a halt.

All these successes would reinforce the fact that I had struck a bargain with Satan. It would just drive me on to get more. But as I said, Satan is a liar. He never failed to win out in the end. After I would get to a certain point, he would disappoint me, and it's just a miracle that I'm sitting here today, and it's a miracle that Jesus Christ later washed my sins, because I actually defiled Him. I said things to and against Jesus that His blood, love and forgiveness just washed and covered. Praise God!

Now I realize that some readers might question my motivations for being so open. I realize that there are some who read these experiences and get nothing out of it except an opportunity to mock and make fun of my ignorance. However because I am a free man today and dead to my own ambitions or reputation, I can say that true confession before God and man brings about a healing, not only in my life, but also in the lives of others. "Confess your faults one to another, and pray one for another that ye may be healed" (James 5 :26). "And they overcame him by the blood of the Lamb, and by the word of their testimony; and they loved not their lives unto the death" (Revelations 12:11).

CANDI SPEAKS: There are so many people today in the same shape as John was. They feel they have no way out of their situation or dilemma. They are involved in witchcraft and don't even know it because drugs constitute a form of sorcery. Even the word 'drugs' originates from the original Greek that gives us our word "pharmaceutical."

You can't play with satan's toys and not be affected. And the psychic line? Don't call it. Leave it alone. It is dangerous because the line is totally operated by demons! A demon always knows what's going to happen to you in the future <u>because he is going to cause it to happen to you.</u>

Wake up world! There is a real enemy out there and he is serious about your soul. Hell was never made for humans, but for satan and his demons. You see, if satan can deceive you into believing him, he will claim your soul. The Bible says that if you yield to God and resist the devil, he will flee from you.

Crack cocaine, cocaine, marijuana, uppers, downers are mind influencing drugs. They are addicting and operative in the realm of your soul (the mind, will and emotions): That's where the problem lies. You and your flesh have absolutely no power over satan. The only power that is more powerful than his power is that which belongs to Jesus Christ, who defeated him on Calvary. Then Jesus gave to those who believe in Him, the power to tread over all the power of satan (Luke 10:19).

Chapter 11

On A Road To No Where

John's escapades with cocaine reoccurred especially when we went to the big cities — Los Angeles, Atlanta — wherever the drug was easy to get.

JOHN SPEAKS: The type of engagements Candi was doing had changed somewhat. We were doing less club dates, because big clubs were closing up. Everybody was discoing. Everybody was a star at a disco, dressed up to play the part. Everybody was living out their fantasy to become a star. All of a sudden this demand was created for Candi to come into these disco joints, and a good number of those clubs were started as gay bars.

CANDI SPEAKS: I was readily accepted by the gay community because of my hit, "Young Hearts Run Free." The gays often felt victimized and they wanted "freedom." So my hit song became an anthem to them.

JOHN SPEAKS: Candi could go into those gay bars, and walk out 30 minutes later with $3,000.00, just for singing those 30 minutes! So, all of a sudden it was more desirable to get into that circuit than it was to put our band together and get in the van, hitch a trailer . . . the whole bit.

John had easy access to cocaine in those clubs. People there could get just about any drug or pill they desired. John would get his cocaine and then disappear. I would be left stranded in hotels because of it. Sometimes he would go to the owner of the club, request the money for our performance, give it back to the owner for coke, and then go, leaving me stranded there. It eventually got to the point where I stopped letting him go out on the road with us. I knew what he was doing; I just didn't know where. I would be so worried about him. When he was like that, he was incoherent and paranoid. He was afraid of his own shadow, afraid that something was after him. Oh, he was so pitiful! But, I knew I couldn't deal with it. John's mother is a psychologist, and she sent him to every major psychologist she knew, and Lord knows, she knew the best ones.

Finally, he got disgusted enough with himself that after one of his "bouts," he checked himself into the hospital. But, that still didn't do any good. His problem was spiritual, not physical or mental. The devil is real, as real as your left arm. The devil doesn't play. You might be playing, but he's not. He's for real. He wants your soul because he's trying to kill you. John 10:10 says, Satan comes "to steal, and to kill, and to destroy." But Jesus said, "I am come that they might have life, and that they might have it more abundantly!"

Here I was, leaning towards divorce again. That's all I knew to do. When a man doesn't work out to suit you, you get rid of him, divorce him. That's how the world thinks, and I was not saved, so I was still thinking like the world. That had always been my pattern. "Don't mope if you can't cope. Get rid of him." I felt sorry for John, though. I really had compassion for him because I knew he was honestly "sick," but what could I do? I couldn't help him, and I was tired of him dragging me down. He was getting embarrassing now. These moments were showing up in public. John would do coke in limousines, or anywhere he could. Yet, Satan was not satisfied just having John. He wanted to kill me, too.

In the spring of 1981, while we were in Los Angeles for a week of engagements, I went through another strange experience that brought this fact home. He and I had gone outside of L.A. in a limousine to do a disco date. After the show John picked up some cocaine that I didn't know about. I had been drinking champagne all night, mixing it with cognac. I had fallen asleep in the limousine on the way back to the hotel. When we got there, John started to snort the cocaine. I got into bed and fell asleep, and I woke up and found him still involved in his coke. I was frantic. "I have told you never to use that stuff in my presence again!" I shouted, but he paid me no attention.

It went on all day. The room seemed damp and cold. It was a strange feeling. I was sitting in the bed, propped up on my pillows. Suddenly, I felt a sharp pain go through my back, straight to my lungs. Something was definitely wrong. Then it went away. In all of my life, I've never had any problems with my lungs. My lungs have always been strong. I had never even had a cough that I could remember.

"Lord, I can't live in here," I wailed. But I couldn't get another hotel room that night because the place was filled. I had no choice but to stay. That night after dinner, I started to cough. I thought it was something that would go away soon, but it didn't. It got worse. It started acting like asthma. Breathing is something we many times take for granted, but I had to concentrate on how each breath was going to come out. I would wheeze all night struggling to get my breath. The devil had attacked my lungs. It came through John inviting him into the room. He was already there, but somehow I opened myself up enough, and he came into my body. I felt like I was going to die from those allergies. We had a trip to South Africa coming up in a week. I was so sick I felt like I was turning blue in the face, trying to breathe. How in the world was I going to sing?

When I got home from L.A., I went to my doctor. He examined me and administered antibiotics, but they didn't help. I kept coughing and coughing, sometimes all night long. I would be up all night, walking the floor. I went to another doctor. He couldn't do anything for me but give me more antibiotics in a pint-size jar, which I took to South Africa with me. I struggled through each show there. Only the Lord knows how I was suffering, trying to do interviews between coughs and act normal.

I got so sick one night, John had to get up at 4:00 in the morning and find me a doctor. The physician came over, examined me, prescribed some medicine, and suggested a vaporizer machine. That didn't help, either. I still kept coughing. So, the next day it was back to his office again. He re-examined me, and this time began to ask me probing questions, like, "What incident took place, when this started?" I told him a little about John's cocaine addictions. "I don't know what this is," he offered, "but it's not 'natural.'" This doctor worked with witch-doctor patients and they had similar ailments, but he could do nothing for me. He felt that the problem was psychosomatic—not physical, but mental. I suffered through five weeks of this.

After we left South Africa, we went to Germany for three weeks. I never had a good day there either. After the tour was over and we went home, I had to go to New York. My mother-in-law heard me coughing, and she said, "I'm going to get you to a respiratory specialist." She made an appointment. That doctor gave me some cortisone and other medicines so I could live with the problem, but a total healing didn't come for another year. On top of the allergy problems, I was still drinking heavily.

For the next year, John and I consistently went downhill. Our relationship was in serious trouble. Professionally, I couldn't even think of the way I was going to deliver a song or do a show. My mind was so preoccupied with John's behavior, knowing that at any given moment he might get up from playing the drums and disappear for three days. I lived in constant fear. I even broke out in a rash worrying about it all.

JOHN SPEAKS: Things got so bad that I entered into an agreement with Candi which enumerated every embarrassing moment that I had put her through, everything that I had done. It said, "These are the things that I have done. I apologize. I will never do these things again . . . ." In it, I explained why I was married to her, and what my motivations were. At the end of it, I wrote, "If I ever do these things again, and cause you embarrassment, you have the right to go and seek an uncontested divorce." I wanted to relieve her of that burden. I really was sincere. I wanted to make my life better, because I began to see that I no longer had control of this. We both signed the contract and she put it away.

I also began to see that if I did lose her, I would have nothing. There was so much of me tied up in her! We shared the same profession; I loved her; we had a marriage. I had a tremendous relationship with all five of her kids. There was just something special about our relationship. So that got me off the hook for the time being, But I still had that drive to sin.

CANDI SPEAKS: It was like John and I were on a merry-go-round, and I couldn't get off. Here was another marriage gone sour.

Chapter 12

Free at Last, Free at Last, Thank God Almighty, I'm Free at Last!

$\mathbf{A}$ll of these events in my life led to a most important day, the day I met Jesus. But there is a difference in being acquainted with someone and really knowing someone. I had been acquainted with Jesus, but I didn't really know Him. I had to learn His ways.

The turning point in my life began after John and I went to a club one night in the spring of 1982. I had been drinking all evening, sitting at the bar, ordering drink after drink. As I sipped one, I fell asleep on the barstool. I almost fell off. I got up to go to the bathroom, knocking over two chairs and clearing a table completely out of my way in the process. I looked around just in time to see John cover his eyes in embarrassment. As I tried to gain composure and dignity to finish my "journey" to the bathroom, I thought, "Enough! I've had it! I've got to quit!" Somehow in my stupor the thought stuck in my mind. I really meant it.

The next day, we went to a park for a picnic. I just couldn't get the thought out of my mind. "I want to quit," I prayed, "but Lord, how? Please God, help me again. I want to change my life. I'm so tired of living this way." I left the family in the park and started to walk alone in the forest. I began to cry. I hadn't cried in a long time. I stopped and sat down on a big rock formation and whispered a prayer. "Lord, somehow make me as strong as this unmovable rock I'm sitting on, and just as solid."

I prayed and meditated for a long time. All of a sudden, I formed a mental picture of my mother's life. I remembered how she used to pray, and when there was a really tough problem, she also fasted. "That's it!" I thought. "I'll fast and pray and I know I'll kick the habit of drinking." "Lord," I vowed, "I'm going to fast and pray until I no longer desire alcohol. I'm through embarrassing my family. I'm tired of being dependent on something. I want to be free."

So I started that Sunday. I was hungover, but I didn't care. I didn't eat or drink water for the next two and a half days. I would say, "God, take the desire away," over and over and over again during those days. On Tuesday evening, after I had prepared dinner for the family, I walked into the bedroom to get away from the food. I heard a voice so clear in my ears I'll never forget the sound. It was so different from my mere mind. The voice, amplified in my ears said, "You can eat now. You are healed." I started to cry and I said, "Oh, thank you Lord!" After regaining my composure, I went back into the kitchen smiling, because I knew I would never drink alcohol again. I was free!

The weekend came. Friends came by with drinks, but I said, "No thank you! I don't care for any." and I really meant it. I would start smiling and couldn't stop. I really didn't want it! Three weeks later, as we prepared to go to Germany for a concert tour, the devil reminded me how cheap alcohol was in that country at the Army bases. We would play at places where drinks were about fifty cents. But I told myself, "I won't be needing any." Sure enough, when we got to Germany, the guys were sending drinks by the tray-full to me backstage. I would give them to the band. I didn't need them.

There in Germany I got dissatisfied with singing the blues. After I sobered up, I started listening to what I was singing. My lyrics were disgusting! I was really getting ashamed to say them. I would get sick each time I had to sing, "I'm a Victim." I began to actually hate that song. I began to dislike "Young Hearts Run Free" as well. "What is happening to Me?" I wondered. I was changing. People would come backstage to say hello, and some would offer a drink. "I don't drink anymore," I would say. "God has delivered me from drinking." They would look at me so strangely.

Now that I think back on it, I was witnessing Jesus. They would quickly get out of the dressing room. I can imagine what they were saying as they went down the halls: "My goodness! These entertainers go from one extreme to another!" I didn't care what they thought. I was just glad to be free! I got to the point that I hated for them to call me on stage. I was turning against show business yet I knew I couldn't stop singing. If I did, I would have no income. So, I reasoned, I was stuck.

I can remember how I began to see people . . . I would be singing and I would look down at them. The people looked so odd to me; they would be so "high" on alcohol or weed or something, their eyes would look weird. I remember saying to myself, "Boy, do they look 'had'!" I continued to study the audience. Some of them would be so drunk they would fall asleep at their tables. I would think, "I'm singing to a bunch of drunks! They don't even appreciate my talents! They hardly know I'm here." I had never noticed it when I was drinking.

I now began to really pay attention to the music as well. I heard every wrong note. Everything was so vivid to me. I don't know how I survived being drunk for five years. I'm so glad Jesus loved me enough to help me gain my sanity. I look back now and know I came through the very gates of hell and God is the one who brought me out.

If you are bound by the same habit, God will deliver you from alcoholism too. He is no respecter of persons, but He does have respect for commitment. Commitment is what He's looking for.

Say, "I'm going to stop!" and mean it! Begin to do something about it! You'll get the help you need. He's waiting on you to make that commitment.

Chapter 13

Enough Is Enough

Only a few months prior to the time that I was delivered from alcohol, John and I had decided that although we kept house in Hanceville, we would rent an apartment in Birmingham. We needed to be more accessible to the airport in Birmingham. We also wanted to be able to socialize with the entertainers that came into town and not have to drive 40 miles at 4:00 A.M... to get home, especially when we might be drunk or high on drugs. We went ahead and got the apartment, though I didn't plan to drink anymore. Nor did I plan on John using cocaine anymore after his written agreement with me!

Only three days after we got our apartment in the city, John suggested that we go to a nightclub. "We haven't been out just to enjoy one another for months," he said. So we went. John remembers that, for a change, he wasn't even looking for cocaine.

JOHN SPEAKS: While at the club, I was playing a video game. This brother that I knew, the boyfriend of one of the backup singers that worked with us, walked up to me.

"Hey, John!" he said to me. "I know somebody who's got some great stuff! You interested?"

I stared at the video game, not looking at him. "Naw, I don't think so, man."

"Wow! That's too bad," he continued.

I wished that he would leave.

"He's just got some stuff, and I know you're good for it. He's willing to give you some. I'll vouch for you. He'll give you some."

Here I had $50.00 in my pocket, but this guy was going to give me some cocaine. I finally looked at him and said, "Well, okay. I'll take a hit."

We went outside, and the man gave it to me, then I went back into the club. "Man! This is great!" I thought to myself. "I got a whole gram from him for nothing!" I had a gram that night, and it wasn't the usual trip.

I stayed up all night. My hobby is photography, and I was planning a photo shoot, snorting cocaine at the dining room table in our apartment. Intermittently Candi would get up, come in, and ask, "Aren't you coming to bed?" Here it was, about 3:00 or 4:00 in the morning. "No!" I snapped, "I don't need to come to bed." About 7:00 in the morning, though, I ran out of the drug. All of a sudden the photography stuff got boring. So, I went to bed. I wasn't asleep 15 minutes before she got up.

CANDI SPEAKS: We had a waterbed, so when John got in bed, I knew it! There was just something in my mind that said, "Go check the dining room table."

Looking back, John explains the ridiculousness of the whole scene. "You get sloppy after so many years!" he says. "The cocaine was on the table and on the rug, too! The drug wasn't as potent as the stuff I usually bought, so it went faster. I'd sniff, and some would fall on the floor or something. I didn't even bother to clean it up. I was using a business card to snort, and that still had some on it. So, after six or seven hours of snorting, there was evidence left!"

I saw a grain here and a grain there that John had left. I stalked back into the bedroom and yelled, "You no-good . . . That's it! I told you! . . ."

John vividly remembers when I stormed in. "I bolted up when she screamed," he says, "and I realized I was in for it. She made her threat good this time. She called a lawyer."

I found one in the yellow pages! Can you believe it? I also called my son, who was living across town. "Get up!" I said. It was 7:00 in the morning. "Come on over here. You've gotta take me down-town!" My blood was boiling. I was screaming. I was ready to tell the world. I had lost all the composure I had been keeping for months. John was sitting there on the bed like he was condemned to die! I was fussing at him and at Marcus. John looked at Marcus, who held up his hand and said, "I'm innocent!" "I'm not taking it anymore!" I screamed. "I'm through! I've taken it for three years. . . ."

I took the agreement we had made to the lawyer and showed it to him. He told me that it wouldn't stand up in court, but I didn't tell John that. I was still going to use it, so I could get a hassle-free divorce. I filed and the divorce papers were drawn up and made ready. My lawyer called me to come and get them.

"That took a week," John recalls. "Meanwhile, during that week, I had no future. So I said, 'What the heck!' I got a check in the mail from my musician's special payment fund. It was a nice size check. I took it directly to the dealer and I bought a whole eighth of an ounce of cocaine. I figured I might as well go down having fun! I was a dummy! Irresponsible! All for the euphoria of the drug."

I was determined not to get pulled down by John. I hadn't had a drink in three months. I was completely dry, and I didn't want to revert back to my drinking, not even to drown my sorrows. "Wednesday, August 3, 1982 — the phone rang, about 9:00 in the morning. It was the lawyer.

"Yeah, I'll do it," I said. "I'll be there."

JOHN SPEAKS: She got off the phone, and said, "It's the lawyer, and he's got the papers prepared. I'm going down to sign them, and I'll be bringing them back for you to sign. Then finally we'll be able to go our separate ways after that.'"

CANDI SPEAKS: As I was leaving, I stopped by the mirror one last time to check my face. Instead, I saw the reflection of John's agony. He was weeping. I turned around to say, "I'll see you later," but I heard that Voice again. The one I heard when I had victory over my alcohol. "You've tried everything else, Candi," He admonished me. "Now try God."

"John," I blurted out, "I don't know why I'm asking you this, but would you consider getting some kind of help? Would you consider going to a man of God and getting some spiritual help?"

At that moment, believe me, as mad as I was at John, my mind was not on God. It was on everything else: "How am I gonna make it? What am I gonna do about startin' my life all over again? I guess I'll meet another fool . . . ." That kind of stuff. I just wanted John to hurry up and answer, so I could get on out of there. And yet I heard this Voice coming through all of this garbage in my mind, saying, "You've tried everything else, now try God." The voice of God was so pure. I looked around and repeated it to John. John said, "I will try anything."

What I said to John I said with authority, and I shocked myself for asking him if he wanted spiritual help. I wondered, "What in the world am I doing this for?" I stood there for a moment, then John said, "What about the church we went to last Sunday? Would you go with me?"

I was surprised again, this time at his answer and his willingness to do what I had suggested. I balked.

"No! I don't need to go with you," I answered arrogantly. He begged me to go with him. I began to think, "Lord, he's never tried the church . . . ." He's tried psychology and psychiatry and all those mind people, but he's never really tried going to church."

"I got on the phone," John recounts, "and called Huffman Assembly of God. I asked to speak to Brother Daniel Ronsisvalle, the pastor. We had gone there the week before out of obligation, because we had said we would go. We had always seen 'Huffman Assembly Presents' on TV Sunday mornings when we came into Birmingham.

He wasn't available, but someone else was. His personal secretary answered the phone, though. "I'd be glad to help you," she said, "but can you give me an idea what the problem is?" So I just told her, "I have a drug-related problem, and it's gotten control of me, and my wife's about to divorce me. I just feel that not only do I need help, but I'm willing to take the steps to get it. And I need to speak to somebody who can help me." The woman said that there was a man there who had experience with drug-related and alcohol-related problems. His name was Ed O'Neal who was the business administrator of the church.

So, I made an appointment with him for 2:00 that afternoon. Here it was, 9:30 in the morning. Over those next three hours, a lot of things happened. I persuaded her to come with me. So Candi rescheduled her appointment with her lawyer for the next day.

Chapter 14

Peace In The Midst Of A Storm

John and I waited in the hall of the church to see Ed O'Neal. I shall never forget some of the things that were going on in my head. "Okay, Candi," I thought. "Here you are back in church. Don't be a sucker again. Remember how you were used when you were little? Churches haven't changed. Watch 'em!"

About that time Brother Ed walked out, introduced himself and led us to his office. As we sat down, I began to look around. It was so peaceful in there! Such a calm! John began to tell Brother Ed more than I had ever dreamed he would tell, because he never shared his deep, dark secrets with anyone. Confession was rolling out, though. John cried as he spoke with him. I just sat there, watching, still kind of angry because I felt John had put me in an awkward situation.

"Here he goes again! Putting me, Candi Staton, the star, through another embarrassing situation." I still had a fat ego. I was still star-struck, haughty, and high-minded, definitely not ready to be humble. Yet I felt something good happening. John told Brother Ed a lot.

"John," Brother Ed counseled, "there's Someone who can free you from that, if you just open up your heart and believe that He can do it." John can best tell about what went on during that all-important conversation:

JOHN SPEAKS: Brother Ed told me about Jesus, and he told me about his own past problems with alcohol dependency. Then he started telling me of a lot of different testimonies of victory that he was aware of in the church. This went on for three hours!

During that time the Lord had shown Brother Ed a vision, but he couldn't understand it. He saw Candi singing to thousands of people, and our lives being a testimony to thousands, for the stand that was going to be made for Jesus. It's funny, because he didn't even know at that time that Candi was a professional singer! He didn't even know her background. So, it was obvious that it was me we were there for.

After Brother Ed had the vision, the conversation changed from me and to Candi, He wanted to find out what Candi did, and that's when her profession came out. He was very frank in saying that anointed, black, soulful type of church singing was very special to him. "Every now and then," he explained, "I feel there's a need in our service to have such singers."

CANDI REMEMBERS: When Brother Ed said that to John and me, my first, smug thought was, "You all don't pay enough for that . . . ." Brother Ed looked at me and said, "Candi, in my vision I saw you singing in the sanctuary. God wants to use you, but you're not ready yet."

"I'll sing some gospel," I answered.

"You're not ready yet," he repeated.

He then turned back to my husband, "John, I've been talking to you for a long time. You're ready to make a decision now. You're at a dead end, man. You can't go on the road you've been going on all these years, and you've gotta make your choice of whether you're going to live for Jesus, and let Him come through you and cleanse you, or whether you're going to continue doing the same old thing.

"If you continue doing the same thing, you're not going to have the opportunity to repent again. I feel in my heart if you walk out of this room, you'll never have the opportunity again to come to the Lord, to have your sins cleansed."

The next few moments became real to John all of a sudden.

JOHN REMEMBERS: I saw that if I made the choice to serve Jesus, even if Candi left me, I wouldn't be alone. My purpose for being there all of a sudden wasn't to keep our marriage going; it was to get a hold on my life.

I saw my life ahead of me, and I wanted to have Jesus live in me. Even if Candi left me, I knew that with Jesus I could make it. So I chose Jesus and opened up my heart, praying the sinner's prayer. Then, I just started bawling! I had never cried like that in my life. All I had ever done in my life, the love of Jesus covered it all. I knew that He had forgiven me!

CANDI REMEMBERS: I began to cry, too — only because I felt sorry for John. I was seeing the same John that cried whenever he did something wrong. I just figured this was another tactic he was using, because he really had to prove himself after that. I knew he had opened up his heart, and I was aware that the minister had prayed for us. But, you've got to realize that I had been in the ministry before. And I knew about "religion." But John didn't. He had been baptized in a Brooklyn, New York, Baptist Church when he was nine. But he says that he had joined the church, not a relationship with Jesus. I told myself, "If this can keep John pacified, then I'm with him." even though I felt it wasn't necessarily a real spiritual experience for him.

After Brother Ed prayed with John and me, he took us on a tour of a recording studio the church had built. Then, he saw us off.

"Candi, give God a chance to heal your marriage. He's already done the work with John," Brother Ed said.

Brother Ed immediately went straight to the intercessors of the church of whom his wife, Edna, was the head. Ed also called the pastor to pray for us. "God wants to use them" he said.

We rode home in silence, lost in our thoughts. When we got to our house, John headed straight for the bedroom, to the drawer where he kept his stash of marijuana. He took it out and headed for the bathroom. He flushed it down the toilet. Then he marched to the kitchen where the beer was, and poured out the cans one by one. There went trouble down the drain!

That made me take a second look. Believe me, I was impressed! I kept thinking, "Oh, he's just trying to impress me, but I know him!" John sat down, skipped supper, and started to read the Gospel of St. John. I was very quiet, thinking, "Is this real, God? I hope so!" I was really interested in seeing John healed so he could stop using so much money, never disappear again, and never leave me stranded again. So I was pleased with what I saw happening; I wanted to use God. This went on for several days.

Wednesday night came, and he was dressing for church when he said, "Come on, Candi. Get dressed!" I slowly got dressed, not really wanting to go, but I went anyway. When we got to the church, John went straight to the front of the sanctuary. I stayed close to the back door.

Then came Sunday, baptismal Sunday. "I'm getting baptized," he told me. "Come on!" I muttered to myself between my teeth. "Don't you think your taking this thing a bit too far?" It didn't matter what I thought! He got baptized!

Wednesday came again and to church we went again. I would always sit near the back, but God was chastening me. I wept during the entire service. There were still questions spinning around in my head. I knew I could never be a Christian and a star, too, so I chose to be a star.

But God and I began to communicate. I could hear a scripture over and over: "Behold, I stand at the door and knock . . ." It was like a broken record. I would sometimes say aloud, "Shut up!" I continued. "Ok, Lord. How am I going to make it if I stop singing in clubs? Who is going to feed my family? You know the family depends on me. Where is the money coming from?"

One night I had tossed and turned all night, unable to sleep. I had booked six weeks of shows starting in September, and I was busy preparing to go on tour, but I was also still under conviction. At the time, we lived in the apartment in Birmingham. I still had my home in the country. I heard that familiar Voice again, saying, "Sell your house. Take the equity and live off of it. I'll supply your needs." I thought for a moment. Then I said, "OK. Send me a buyer." Interest rates were sky high. The house was better than any house in the whole area. I knew nobody would want to invest in it.

Only two days later a retired school teacher called me and asked me if she could see the house. She wanted to buy it! I had already formed in my mind the amount of equity I would ask for. Before I could tell her, she said, "I can only give you this amount." She gave me a figure, and it was exactly the figure I wanted to ask for. That closed the deal. The bank refinanced, brought the interest rates very low for her, and we closed—in a week! God worked a miracle! He is so real!

We got the check, but I was still determined to go on tour. I had the money, but I figured, "If I have the money from the tour, we could budget right and live comfortably for a while." But that's not the way God works. He wants us to walk by faith. I knew my reasoning was wrong, but I kept on planning the trip. Then I realized I hadn't heard the scriptures in my head for the past few days. It was total silence. It sort of bothered me, but I kept on planning.

On Thursday night, after being restless all evening, I got up to go to the store. All of my kids were at our apartment. I kept looking for one of my sons to drive me to a convenience store, but I couldn't find anyone. So I decided to drive myself. I jumped in the van and started to the store.

At one point, I was about to turn left when, I saw some oncoming traffic. I felt I had enough time to cross the street. As soon as I made my turn I felt an impact. I was knocked completely out of the driver's seat, into the passenger's seat behind the captain's chair on the other side. The impact was so hard, that the van rocked from side to side, as if trying to decide if it wanted to turn over. I was scared. All the lights came on in the van, because the door was knocked open. The impact had also turned the van completely around, headed in the opposite direction. "Jesus! Oh, help me Jesus!" I found myself screaming at the top of my voice. "I'm sorry, Lord!" I repented. I was shaking. Then I heard God's voice again. He said, "Get up. Get under the wheel. Park the van." But the van was already parked, out of the way of the traffic. All I had to do was turn the ignition off.

I sat there for awhile, just shaking. When I got out to walk to a phone and call the police, two teen-age girls stopped me. "Where did that guy come from?" they asked. "We saw it all. He came from nowhere! When we looked, he was running into you!" The driver of the other car was bleeding, and his car was totaled. The motor had been knocked out of it. Finally the police came and wrote the accident up.

It was all a humbling experience. God really knows how to humble you! After they asked their questions, I left for home. When I got home with the van, it looked terrible! I couldn't stop shaking. After all the excitement had died down and everybody had gone to bed, I was still up, reliving the accident. I got scared all over again. It was awful. Finally I went to bed. I tossed and turned, so I said, "Lord, please get this accident out of my mind so I can sleep." In a few minutes I fell asleep.

An hour later I woke up again. God spoke to me and said, "Get the Bible." So, I got it and went into the living room. My hands turned the pages, but I had no idea what passage I was going to. "Lord, where do you want me to read?" I prayed. My hand stopped at Isaiah 42:6.

"I, the Lord, have called thee in righteousness and will hold thine hand." I read on, until the 10th verse really got my attention. In it, God said, "Sing unto the Lord a new song and his praise from the end of the earth."

I sat there a long time, just crying. I couldn't stop crying. Then the Lord said to me, "I could have taken your life tonight, but I want to use you." He said, "I have the keys to hell and death in my hands. I spared your life tonight for a reason." I humbled myself that night. I got on my knees by the living room couch and confessed all of my sins to God, then asked Jesus personally into my heart. And He came! I couldn't stop crying. I made God a promise then and there, that I would sing His praises. I would live for him, I would walk in His ways, and I would be obedient. I meant every word. When I got in the bed again, I was a new creature. Old things had passed, and behold all things were new.

Later that morning, I woke up refreshed. I had never felt so clean in all of my life. I got on the phone and began to cancel shows. All of them. From that point on, John and I were in church every time they had a service. We both sat near the front. We were so hungry for the Word of God, we couldn't get enough! We would study at home and go to church, then come home and discuss the service and study some more.

I started to love God's Word. I had never understood the Bible in my entire life. Now it was all becoming clear to me. God revealed more and more of Himself to me. I loved it. John and I didn't do anything for six months except study. That's when I started to write songs. I was home alone every day, and I would write and write all the time, beautiful songs! I wrote, "Sin Doesn't Live Here Anymore" in that time. We wanted to check out the sound in the studio at the church, so we recorded a demo of the song. I just couldn't stop playing it. It was one of the most beautiful songs I'd ever heard!

Chapter 15

Sin Doesn't Live Here Anymore

I had a lot of forgiving to do even after I got saved. I began to really search my heart, deep down inside, and the Lord showed me that I had to forgive my ex-husbands. I thought I had already forgiven them but I was wrong. I wasn't totally healed of the frustrations and the things I lost by being married to them. I still blamed them for my not being farther along on the road to success. I always believed in my heart, "If it had not been for so and so, I would be here or there."

I gave it up to Jesus allowed Him to heal the hurts and the accusations. I know now if some of those things had not happened to me, I would not have been in the ministry today. I can rejoice because I suffered afflictions for a reason. That reason is sitting in heavenly places with my Lord. If it took all of that to get me to this point, then I say, "Praise the Lord!"

Another thing changed after I had accepted Jesus as my Savior. I made a vow to Him. I would never, ever sing any more secular songs. I don't believe God needs help from the devil to make anyone "successful." I just couldn't see myself singing in nightclubs on Saturday and church on Sunday. The Word says, "A double-minded man is unstable in all of his ways." I didn't want to be a hypocrite. I knew that God loves "all or nothing people." (read Revelation 3:15-16).

Vows are made for keeping. After making that vow to Him, though, I don't think I fully realized exactly what I had done. It was like a contract between me and God. I called up the club owners and tried to explain to them what I had done. Some of them made a joke out of it. Some hung up on me. One guy threatened to sue because I canceled a show. Friends began to call and challenge me as to why I was doing this. Some thought it was just a phase. Nobody fully realized what was "wrong" with me. I remember when I first got "saved," one man told me on the phone, "I acted like you, but it soon wore off. I'll give you a few months. It'll wear off."

Well, my spirits were high, but my money was getting low. There was absolutely no money coming in. John and I had laid our talents on the altar and said, "If you want to use us, Lord, we give these talents to you. Please anoint them and give them back to us." So John went out and found a job selling insurance, and I was at home all day by myself, with a lot of time on my hands. I was continually seeking God. He said, "If you seek Me with all your heart, you shall find Me."

One day shortly after we had recorded the demo of "Sin Doesn't Live Here Anymore," my agent called me from New York. He had booked a show for me in Miami and had already collected the money.

"You can send the money back," I responded, even though I didn't have much money left at that time. "I have given my life to Jesus. I'm not singing the blues anymore."

He angrily hung up on me. When he did, I lifted my hand and started praising God. At that time the Holy Spirit fell like a rushing, mighty wind, and filled the place where I was standing. I felt like I was being ruptured! It felt like I had been shocked by electricity, but it was all over me, especially in my mouth, from which a beautiful language flowed. Praise God!

I couldn't wait to tell John, because he hadn't received the baptism of the Holy Spirit yet, and he was so desirous for this gift. But John is very intellectual. He had attended Harvard University and was a scientist by trade. He tried to figure everything out logically. You can't figure God out! His ways are not like our ways and His thoughts are higher than ours. (Isaiah 55:8-9). "Guess what!" I exclaimed when John came home. I began to tell him what had happened to me. I could see the longing in his eyes, so I started to pray for him.

I began praying in the Spirit every day. I didn't realize what I was doing, because I hadn't had any teaching on this subject. I surely was getting a kick out of hearing that language I couldn't understand! I didn't realize at the time that I was fighting in a spiritual realm.

You see, "we wrestle not against flesh and blood," Paul says, "but against . . . spiritual wickedness in high places" (Ephesians 6:12). If you read the 10th chapter of Daniel, it will give you an idea how you can be stopped in another realm, which is above you spiritually. The devil is in that realm, stopping you if he can, and your prayers won't get through. But when you pray in the Spirit, you battle with the devil with more power than the devil's got. You win every time.

I didn't realize at that time in our life that financial success comes from God, because I had been taught, "You've got to be poor and pitiful if you want to get to heaven, 'cause heaven will be worth it all, Honey!" I didn't know you had to do battle with the devil for your finances like you do for your health. This is when I got a visitation from God. I had been fasting off and on since I received the baptism, but I heard God speak clearly one morning as I was waking up.

"I want you to go on a long fast," he said.

"God is this You? If it's really You, show me what You want me to do."

The following night I had a dream. In it, my nephew and his wife came into a big auditorium, it reminded me of the stage at the Palladium in London. The band I had was setting up the stage. It looked like we were about to do a concert. They walked up on the stage and handed me a picnic basket wrapped in a white linen napkin. Inside the picnic basket was a bottle of pills, written in longhand, as it is done in Europe. On this white bottle was black writing that said, "Take one three times a day; fasting and prayer for ? days." It had the amount of days, but when I woke up I couldn't remember the number. Now I know why. I would have been counting the days instead of praying like I should.

"When shall I start?" I asked Him.

"After communion Sunday night," He answered. I didn't know we were having communion on Sunday night, but we sure did.

So that's when I started my fast. I had a lot of things to seek God for.

For one, I wanted John filled with the Holy Spirit. Also, we tried to get on record labels, but nobody seemed interested. Every door seemed closed to us, and we had no money. John was earning some, but not nearly enough to support us. I was not known in the gospel field enough for churches to want me. Nobody really knew me as well as I was known in the pop world. A lot of Christians just don't listen to secular music, so they didn't know who Candi Staton was. Meanwhile, my disco people were calling me to do some disco dates.

My bills were piling up, so the devil was telling me, "You know you need the money. Go ahead and do the dates. Nobody will ever know."

"Shut up!" I retorted. "God will know!" I kept praying, "God, You said You'll never leave me or forsake me. Help me God, please. I don't want to make You ashamed. You said I would never be ashamed." Oh, how I sought God! My kids were in school, and I hardly had lunch money to give them.

Businesses were starting to sue us for nonpayment. I used to hate to hear John explain our financial situation to creditors. I would be so embarrassed because I was used to having more than enough money. John hated to try to explain it all to them as well.

"We got saved and we've stopped working in nightclubs, so our income was cut off. Now we are making our record," he said. "As soon as the record comes out, I will try to catch up. Please be patient with us. We are not trying to run from our responsibilities, but when you are called to the ministry, you have to go. I hope you understand our position."

"Sure!" they must have thought. "These guys are out of their tree!" Little did we know we would also have to fight, even in the gospel arena — traditional and contemporary. We had yet to find out that Satan is still in some of that. If you are really committed, you will find opposition.

Anyway, Monday came and I started my fast. I told John. He said, "You better be sure God told you, if you are going on a long one." That Monday was the hardest day of my life. I got so hungry! But I just kept drinking water rather than eating. I can remember preparing a good meal for the family and the aroma was so strong! The whole house smelled like food! I felt like eating the throw pillows on the couch! I went to my bedroom and I prayed, "Ok, God. Make the hunger go away." Sure enough, I was all right. So, I got through day one.

Day two was a little better, but it was still rough. On the third day I began to get weak. I said, "God, give me joy," and my strength began to come back. Early on the fourth day, John went to the studio to mix our "Make Me an Instrument" album, my first for the Lord. I was left all alone in the apartment and I woke up to a refrigerator that was iced up. I couldn't open the freezer, so I got out a knife, hot water, a mop, a broom and towels. But, I surely didn't feel like defrosting the refrigerator! I hadn't eaten in four days!

Here I was in the middle of a puddle in the kitchen floor, really mad. I started talking to God loudly. "Ok, God," I said sternly. "You said for me to come out of the nightclubs. I did... I was making good money, too. But, I did what you said. Now, I'm over here starving to death! My family is suffering. Do you honestly think this is fair? Speak to me! I know you are up there."

I ranted and raved for a few minutes before I just broke. "I'm sorry, God," I said, broken. "I'm so sorry I spoke to you like that." I started crying. "I'll go through anything I have to... please forgive me." I didn't know at the time that God says in Isaiah 43:26, "Put me in remembrance; let us argue our case together. State your cause, that you may be proved right."

There was nothing wrong with us arguing, and I didn't know then that the Lord was letting us do just that, and the blessings from it were about to come. I dropped my mop and raised my hands. Tears were streaming by now. God came into that kitchen in the form of a whirlwind and I felt I was spinning in the middle of it. He began to speak to me.

"The earth is mine, and the fullness thereof, the world and those that dwell therein," He said. "I know you. I know what you seek, and I'm here to answer all of your prayers. I want you to know that I am bigger than you ever pictured me. Nobody has ever captured my image. Stop thinking that I can't perform my Word!"

By now my body felt limp, but His power came upon me and shook me until my teeth chattered. I couldn't stop, and I didn't want to stop. I was in the very presence of God. There was a strange heat energy all over the room, God's voice. I can only try to explain it as best as I know how. It was like liquid and it was all over me. It wasn't audible. It was in my hands and arms, my head, my ears were amplified. I felt like I had speakers in my eardrums. I was running, spinning, jumping, and screaming at times. I saw images. There was a brightness. I had furniture in the kitchen, dining room, and living room. I never opened my eyes for a long time, but I was moving all around those areas, never bumping into anything.

God's presence is so real! I began to ask God to stay His hand, because my flesh could not take much more of this. I spoke in at least seven different languages. I would speak in one, and my stomach was pulsing. I would try to stop, crying, "Oh, Jesus! I love you" Then I would begin to speak in another tongue. All the time He was talking to me. I can't remember everything He said, but He confirmed His words, mostly in scripture.

"I am sending you two men to help you," He said.

As He spoke to me, Mike Murdock's face came into view like on a TV screen, then the other man, Brother Ed O'Neal, who led us to the Lord.

"They will help you."

This went on from 11 A.M. until 1 P.M. I began to praise God that His presence would overshadow me again, again and again.

When you're in the very presence of God, there is no doubt. I didn't question anything the Lord was saying to me. I had perfect faith. I knew whatever He said was going to happen. I felt very bold. I wasn't self-conscious or embarrassed, even though I wasn't being quiet and was surrounded by people living beside me, over me and under me in my apartment.

The presence of God is perfection. Everything is perfect. There is fullness of joy. No fear is there, no sickness is there. Everything is perfect. That's the way heaven is. I really didn't want to come out of that precious time with the Lord. I wanted to stay in His presence.

I was so enraptured in God's precious presence, I remember saying to God, "Please let John feel what I am feeling right now."

Immediately the request was granted.

Chapter 16

God Will Never Let You Fail

While everything was happening to me at the apartment, John was having lunch with Noah White, our engineer at Spectrum Studios. John was mixing the "Make Me an Instrument" album. As they sat down at a restaurant table, a most unusual sequence of events began to take place for them.

The waitress came over, took their orders, smiled and joked with them. She then headed for the kitchen, only to walk back to them with a puzzled look on her face.

"Excuse me," she said. "I hope you don't think I'm stupid, but God spoke to me. You are a drummer, aren't you? God said, you play His music, and you are seeking something, aren't you? You are seeking the baptism of the Holy Ghost, right?"

John never got a chance to answer any of her questions. She was just asking and answering away. Noah's eyes were big and puzzled by now. So were John's, for that matter! None of them knew that I was having a visitation from the Lord at the same time she spoke to them in the restaurant.

"I would lay hands on you right now to receive the Holy Spirit," she explained, with tears flowing down her cheeks, "but I might lose my job! Plus there's too much unbelief in here, these people wouldn't understand. Where will you be about 2 p.m.?"

"I will be in the studio in that church right across the street," he said pointing in that direction.

"Ok, I'll be there at 2 o'clock."

She went to wait on another table, and John and Noah finished their memorable lunch hour.

Right at 2:00 pm, just as they planned, the woman arrived at the studio. The woman and John went into one of the rooms while Noah stood in the doorway watching. I'm sure he was still puzzled as to what was going on. She laid hands on John and began praying. John says he felt his feet begin to tingle as the Holy Spirit began to enter him. Then, a warmth flooded all the way up his legs to his body. When it got to his face, his jaw began to tremble. Very simple words started to flow, sounding much like a baby's first words.

Back at the apartment, I was resting on the couch following my visitation from the Lord. I was to be sore for days afterwards. John called to tell me what had just happened to him. It was one of the most exciting days of his life. I couldn't believe everything was happening so fast. My life was changing dramatically in one day! As soon as it was over, Ed O'Neal called.

"God told me to help you," he said. "What do you need?"

This was incredible!

Later that evening, about 6:00, Brother Dan Ronsisvalle, our pastor, called. "Mike Murdock is coming in today on business. I told him about you all, and he wants to see you. Can you come over here tonight after he finishes his meeting?"

"Just tell us when!" I replied.

"I'll call you when he's finished," he said. "Stand by the phone."

I still couldn't figure out what part Mike Murdock would play in this drama that was unfolding. He was the composer of the theme song for The Jim Bakker Show, "You Can Make It", on the PTL Television Network. He also was a frequent guest on the show. Brother Dan called at 9:30p.m. We drove to the church to meet Mike for the first time and played a couple of the songs I had written. He was blessed.

"The world needs to hear your testimony," he said. He got out his briefcase and began to write a letter to Jeannie Johnson at the

PTL Television Network, recommending us for the Jim Bakker Show.

God had already revealed to us long before this incident that he wanted us to have our own record label, but we really didn't want that responsibility. Being from the secular arena, I knew the headaches of working with most record companies. "Thanks, God," I had said, "but no thanks!" Instead, we kept trying to get on a record label. We were in negotiations with one of the biggest in gospel music. We kept waiting for something to happen with them. Shortly after the visitation, they called. But we could not come to an agreement. We were still trying to hold on to something we could see, yet God wanted us to fully trust him.

PTL wrote us a nice letter after they received our package. "We are impressed," it said. "God bless you and your ministry." That was it.

As long as you hold on to anything, you can't receive God's best, and God wants you to have His best. We had one thing we were still holding on to. We still had our eyes on something other than God. God wanted me to totally trust and depend on Him. So he made it impossible to sign with that record company. God knew if that record company had seen us on "The Jim Bakker Show," they probably would have been more lenient towards us. But, instead, they gave us a deal we could not accept. In fact, it was the worse deal I've ever heard of in all my years of negotiating contracts! And God knows I've seen a few deals in my career! I had to say no, even though we were down to our last $50.00 in the bank.

"Oh Lord, it's all on you now," I prayed. "I'm standing in the middle of the ocean, and if I'm going down, I'm going down with you. I have no more strings. I'm all yours to do what you want."

That's when things started - after we made that decision. I was up all night praying that prayer. At about 4:00 that morning, I had the TV on the PTL Network. Mike Murdock was on and he sang a song called, "God Will Never Let You Fail." The tears started. I felt God was with me. I had peace, real peace. A peace I had never known before and I went to sleep.

I was awakened by the phone later that morning. It was Jeannie Johnson.

"How fast can you all get to PTL?" she asked. "We need you this week."

At that, we danced all over the room, praising God!

Things started changing for us after the visit to Jim Bakker's program. We had put our "Make Me an Instrument" album out on our own Beracah label, with a custom-type cover. That was all we could afford.

"I want to help you. I want our company to do what it can for you," Jim said.

We could hardly believe all this was happening so quickly. We made a deal with Eric AuCoin at PTL Records and Tapes to distribute Beracah Records, our label. I love Jim Bakker. He has helped so many people get started in their ministries. After that, churches started calling us to come and minister. Finances began to come in. Our records began to sell. God was prospering us. Now I know why God insisted we have our own label. It was so we could have a cushion for our ministry. He is so smart! Why can't we always trust Him? We trust the devil, but we won't trust God!

I used to travel thousands of miles, going to some town I had never been to before, to some promoter I had never seen in my life. Yet I trusted their word! They could have gone off in left field on me and left me stranded. Some of them did. Yet I continued to trust them. Why couldn't I trust God? God's Word is always true. He's never left any of us. We've always left Him. He's never lied, but we've lied to Him. I know I did. He keeps His part of the bargain. We're the ones who break the vows, yet He's still merciful. God has a lion personality – Lion of Judah (judgment) and a lamb personality (grace).

The lion personality is described in the Old Testament, and the lamb personality is in the New Testament. I wonder sometimes how long will it be before we provoke Him to anger, and we see the lion personality in action. "Woe unto those that fall into the hands of an angry God," the scripture says. Jesus said, "I am the same yesterday and today and forevermore" (Hebrews 13:8).

Chapter 17

Jesus, the Same Today, Yesterday and Forever

So many exciting things have happened since I gave my life totally to Jesus. For one thing, God gave me a real husband in John. In my heart I always knew what kind of husband I wanted. I searched and searched for him, but for so long was unable to find him. Each husband had some of the qualities, but since his conversion, John has all of the qualities. Now, I couldn't ask for a more complete husband, and I give God all the praise.

God called John into the pastorate. He is the founder and pastor of Upon This Rock Family Church in Atlanta, Georgia. He is also the President of Beracah Records, heading up not only the ministry and record company, but also our publishing company. He is extremely talented in running the ministry and the business God has given us stewardship over.

Until God saved my husband, he never used all the education he acquired while he attended Milton Academy and Harvard University. Now he's using all those skills for God. It's so amazing how the Lord always knows and saves the best part of our lives for Himself. God has really blessed us in this ministry. It is growing by leaps and bounds.

Our first Christian album, "Make Me an Instrument", was nominated for a Grammy Award in 1984. Since then, we have recorded seven albums. We are also doing a lot of television now, we had our own TV show on the Trinity Broadcasting Network called "New Direction." It was shown internationally via satellite. That show was canceled for one year. Now we have a new TV show called "Say Yes To Life" which is aired weekly on Trinity Broadcasting Network. After being frequently on TBN, well-known evangelists began to call us to do camp meetings, seminars, and crusades. That's how I got involved with Word of Faith Church in Dallas, Texas in the late spring of 1985.

I'll never forget how I felt the first night I walked upon the platform to sing there. The presence of the Holy spirit was so strong! I had sung my songs a lot of times, but there was a real difference in them that night. When Brother Norvel Hayes began to teach on the gifts of the Spirit, things began to happen. People saw angels walking past them. One 14 year-old boy was taken into a vision in which he saw a brightness and words coming over a hill: "Prosperity," "Healing," "Deliverance." The fourth grade class of Word of Faith Christian School asked their teacher that Monday morning if they could stay in and pray instead of going out to recess -- which is a miracle! Some of them went into a trance and saw angels walking in the classrooms, and when they came out they all described the angels they saw. Each child had the same description.

Valerie Owens, one of the Bible school instructors, also was taken into a trance that morning, paralyzed for over an hour. She saw the revival that was taking place. That was the beginning of a 60-day revival that I was a part of. I remember one night God's cloud of glory came into the altar area of the church. It was so thick, it looked like smoke. I asked God, "What was that?" He had me turn to Revelations 15:8, which read, "The temple was filled with smoke from the glory of God and His power." Then the profile of Jesus appeared on the big air conditioning vent. The first night it appeared I knew I had never seen anything so clear.

Needless to say, it was exciting to be a part of that great revival. So many miracles happened! Cancer patients walked away healed, confirmed by their doctors. Blind eyes were opened. Two people were raised from the dead . . . I could write another book about the miracles alone, The biggest miracle of all was that hundreds of souls were saved. I know I was revived; I'll never be the same since the revival. God still visits His people!

I know the hand of God is on us and He guides us in everything that we do. When I started to write this book several years ago, I never thought about publishing it until the Lord began to chastise me. I want to share with you what the Lord has shown concerning music.

I decided when I got saved that I would take an uncompromising stand and was going to do so no matter what. Sometimes you have to stand alone, but nevertheless stand! The Word says, having done all, to stand.

I came out of a world of entertainment, where people will do most anything just to get airplay, including giving away drugs and money. It's called "payola." Competition was out of control. People pushed to get Grammy Awards, music awards and any kind of recognition they could get.

I was shocked to find the same thing happening in Christian circles. Some gospel singers, and musicians that I admire and love have literally sold Jesus out for 30 pieces of silver, including the cross, the anointing and the blood. If we don't preach the gospel, who will? We have become too world-conscious. We want to identify and blend with the world. When I say "world," I don't mean the world Jesus was speaking about when He said go into all the "world" and preach the gospel. I'm talking about the secular scene, the party scene.

Some radio stations won't play records that talk about the Blood, the Name of Jesus, the Cross, and all, because it might offend the religion of someone who doesn't believe in Jesus.

"We have to sell records to the entire religious communities and secular communities as well, which includes New Age, Buddhists, Muslims and more." The bottom line is record sales. The music director at a radio station told me he couldn't play our records because my lyrics were too strong. Now how can the Blood of Jesus, the cross and His return be too strong? Are we still singing the gospel or not? It really grieves me to know what the devil is doing in gospel music. The big record labels have gotten into gospel music because it's a new market and it will make money. That's their only interest. They are not interested in Jesus and Him crucified. As a matter of fact, they don't even believe in Jesus.

Jesus told us to preach the gospel, saying "The kingdom of Heaven is at hand. Heal the sick, raise the dead, cast out demons" and shout it on the house tops that He is coming soon. Christian radio stations will play your music if the sound is contemporary pop. Airplay results if the lyrics say "light" instead of "Lord," "Love" instead of "Jesus," and then perhaps, the name can be slipped in without somebody knowing it. If listeners are scanning stations, they will perhaps stop if the lyrics are not "too strong." What kind of witness is that, especially when considering some of the saints have gone on to glory after having given their lives for the gospel of Jesus Christ?

Paul said, "I am not ashamed of the gospel of Jesus Christ for it is the power of God unto salvation to every one that believeth." How can you believe something if you don't know what somebody is talking about? They call it a positive message. Well, every message has a sender. Who sent the message anyway? Some people say they don't want to offend anyone. I would rather have someone's feelings hurt than for them to go to hell. I think that compromise is an abomination before God. Isaiah 58:1 says, "Cry aloud and spare not, lift up your voice as a trumpet and show my people their transgressions and the house of Jacob their sins."

I'll be the first to admit the message of Jesus Christ is not a popular message. I don't care how contemporary you make it, it's still not popular. A student is not above his teacher. Jesus said if He was persecuted, we will be persecuted too. Study the life of Jesus, and that's how your life should be. He left the example for us to follow. If He was spit on, we will be too, scorned, so will we, mocked, so will we. That doesn't bother me. I knew when I gave my life to Jesus it would be a faith walk. That's why it took me so long to make a decision. But, when I did, I knew what I was in store for. I had to decide whether I wanted fame and fortune or to take up my cross and follow Jesus. For I knew I had to walk according to God's Word and not according to the world. If you don't fully make up your mind, you run the risk of confusing people.

I meet so many young people who are confused about the double message they are getting. They see their favorite gospel singers testifying they are "born again" and they put out several gospel albums. Their pictures are on the covers of contemporary Christian magazines. Then you turn on M.T.V. and they are singing secular music and shaking everything God gave them. I often counsel those young people and pray with them. I usually take them to 2 Cor. 6:14, "Be not unequally yoked together with unbelievers for what fellowship has righteousness with unrighteousness and what communion hath light with darkness."

Also, James 3:10-12 says, "Out of the same mouth proceedeth blessings and cursings. My brethren these things ought not to be. Doth a fountain send forth at the same place sweet and bitter? Can a fig tree, my brethren, bear olive berries, either a vine, figs? So can no fountain yield both salt and fresh water." The 13th verse sums it all up: "Who is a wise man endued with knowledge among you. Let him show a good conversation his works with meekness of wisdom."

James is saying that you should have a good life-style. Don't be a foolish person. You will be held responsible for the lives you lead astray. Jesus said it would be better that a mill stone be hung around your neck and dropped into the sea than to harm or lead astray one of His little ones. We, as gospel singers and Christians, have an awesome responsibility. We are role models whether we want to be or not. People pattern themselves after us. Therefore, we must stay clean and unspotted from the world. God let me know my job description one day as I was asking, "Lord what part do I play in the Body of Christ?" He said, "You are a psalmist." I began to study the role of a psalmist.

TO THE PSALMISTS:

Numbers 8:6: "Take the Levites from among the children of Israel and cleanse them."

This was God speaking to Moses. God chose the Levites to be his special people. They were like an offering to the Lord. They were totally separated from the children of Israel because they were set apart for the service of the sanctuary. The Levites were ordained to handle the Ark of the Covenant. Along with the priests, they handled the very presence (Glory) of God. The Levites were praisers. They would go into the temple and sing praises.

There were three leaders, Asaph, Heman and Jeduthon. They each had eight hour shifts to stay in the temple to praise God. So, the temple was never idle. There were praises going on 24 hours a day.

God chose the Levites because they refused to compromise. When Moses was upon the mountain receiving the Ten Commandments from God, the devil persuaded the children of Israel to disbelieve God by getting Aaron to make an idol, a golden calf, and convinced them that the calf brought them out of Egypt. The Levites would have no part in that, but rather rebuked them. When Moses came off the mountain and said, "Who is on the Lord's side?" the Levites were the first to come over to Moses. God saw that and honored that. Therefore, God entrusted the holy things to the Levites.

What does that have to do with us today? Jesus said, "I didn't come to destroy the law but fulfill it. When we get saved by asking Jesus into our lives and then receive the infilling of the Holy Spirit, we receive power. Then, praise is born out of our spirits. We become His sanctuary. We become like Asaph, Heman and Jeduthon. We praise God hour after hour in our hearts. Our very being praises God. That's why David, the chief psalmist, said, "His praise shall continually be in my mouth."

There is also an office of the psalmist. Asaph, Heman and Jeduthon stood in the office of the psalmist. It is the oldest office in the church. I believe that is why when we assemble ourselves together to worship, we always start by singing. Even before evangelists, teachers, pastors, apostles and prophets were ever established in the New Testament, there was always the office of the psalmist ushering in the Glory of God in the temple.

I believe that's why Paul didn't name the psalmist along with the five-fold ministry, because it was common knowledge to everyone. It had been around for centuries. I believe that's one reason the office of the psalmist is so anointed. 2 Chronicles 5:13 describes how the cloud would come into the temple while the Levites were praising God, and the priests could not stand to minister because of the cloud. The very Glory of God would fill the place.

That is the reason Satan attacks God's music so viciously. First of all, he is jealous because that was once his position, and he knows first-hand how anointed it is. He, as we all know, was created by God to lead praise and worship in Heaven. Before Satan became proud and was kicked out of Heaven, he was the "Anointed Cherub" that covers. He had a built-in band in his body (Ezekiel 28). Satan is smart enough to know that the anointing breaks the yokes. So, he will deceive and distract you from praising and worshipping God.

Singing the name of Jesus, encompasses all the names of Jehovah, Jehovah Rapha-Healer, Jehovah Shalom-Peace, Jehovah Jireh-Provider, Jehovah Rohi-Shepherd, Jehovah M'Kaddesh-Sanctifier, Jehovah Tsidkenu-Righteousness, and Jehovah Shammah-Present. All of His characteristics come forth.

I have seen healings take place in my own services. Epileptics healed, backs snapped back into place, confusion leaves, migraine headaches go, female problems vanish, lesbians totally set free, cigarette habits broken, breech babies turned around in their mother's womb, demons of fear leave, and that's just to name a few. Why? Because the anointing is there. The presence of Almighty God is in our midst. Anything can happen when He is there. Don't come to our services to be entertained, although you will be. But, rather, come looking for Jesus. You will find Him, and you won't leave like you came.

The anointing rests upon a person whose life is totally yielded to God. You might have a beautiful talent or gift but God won't anoint it until you yield yourself to Him. The Bible says the gift of God is without repentance. Secular singers and musicians have a gift, but unfortunately it is wrapped in selfish ambition and foolish pride, and many other things, money – a big name, or merely to see your name up in lights. I know; that's the way I was before asking Jesus to come into my life.

The Spirit of God is awesome. He only dwells in clean and holy places. When Moses and Joshua were coming from the mountain, the children of Israel were dancing and singing. Joshua thought something good had happened. He said, "Listen, Moses, I hear singing." Moses said, "It is not the voice of those who shout in victory, nor is it the voice of those who cry in defeat, but the voice of those who sing. Here he meant entertainment. They were drunk and dancing, singing around the idol they had made. Moses became angry that he threw the Ten Commandments at them and destroyed a big portion of them. God is the same today, yesterday and forever. When it comes to holiness, God is very serious. I often say before I speak, I am a serious person, doing a serious work, for a serious God!

I pray this book has been an inspiration to you, and I pray right now for everyone who reads this book that God may use you and keep you in the palm of his hand, so that you can be meet for the Master's use.

To those of you who want to know the Lord, I want to lead you into a simple prayer, "The word is nigh you, even in your mouth and in your heart (that is the word of faith which we preach): That if you confess with your mouth the Lord Jesus and believe in your heart that God has raised Him from the dead, ye will be saved. For with the heart one believes unto righteousness and with thy mouth confession is made unto salvation (Romans 10:8-10).

Simply repeat this prayer, "Lord Jesus, I know I am a sinner. I confess my sins to you right now. Please forgive me and come into my heart. Make me a new creation. I believe that you are the Son of God, that you died on a cross and rose from the dead, and are now seated at the right hand of the father. Thank you Jesus for coming into my heart. I now know I am saved."

God Bless You,
Candi

Music by Candi Staton

Title

Make Me An Instrument (#1001)	Cassette only	
The Anointing (#1010)	Cassette only	
Sing A Song (#2001)	Cassette only	
Love Lifted Me (#2010)	Cassette only	
Stand Up And Be A Witness ((#2020)	Cassette	CD
Standing On The Promises (#2040)	Cassette	CD
I Give You Praise (#2060)	Cassette	CD

Master Card, Visa, Check & Money Orders Accepted:
Please Do Not Send Cash

$10.00 for cassettes
$12.00 for CD's
add $2.00 per item for shipping and handling

Send orders to:

Candi Staton
Beracah Ministries, Inc.
Post Office Box 2265
Norcross, Georgia 30091-2265
(404) 587-4861

OTHER BOOKS FROM
Pneuma Life Publishing

Why?
by T.D. Jakes

Why do the righteous, who have committed their entire lives to obeying God, seem to endure so much pain and experience such conflict? These perplexing questions have plagued and bewildered Christians for ages. In this anointed and inspirational new book, Bishop T.D. Jakes provocatively and skillfully answers these questions and many more as well as answering the "Why" of the anointed. ***Also available as a workbook***

Water in the Wilderness
by T.D. Jakes

Just before you apprehend your greatest conquest, expect the greatest struggle. Many are perplexed who encounter this season of adversity. This book will show you how to survive the worst of times with the greatest of ease, and will cause fountains of living water to spring out of the parched, sun–drenched areas in your life. This word is a refreshing stream in the desert for the weary traveler.

The Harvest
by T.D. Jakes

Have you been sidetracked by Satan? Are you preoccupied with the things of this world? Are you distracted by one crisis after another? You need to get your act together before it's too late! God's strategy for the end-time harvest is already set in motion. Phase One is underway, and Phase Two is close behind. If you don't want to be left out tomorrow, you need to take action today. With startling insight, T.D. Jakes sets the record straight. You'll be shocked to learn how God is separating people into two distinct categories. One thing is certain – after reading *The Harvest,* you'll know exactly where you stand with God. This book will help you discover who will and who won't be included in the final ingathering and determine what it takes to be prepared. If you miss *The Harvest,* you'll regret it for all eternity!

Help Me! I've Fallen
by T.D. Jakes

"Help! I've fallen, and I can't get up." This cry, made popular by a familiar television commercial, points out the problem faced by many Christians today. Have you ever stumbled and fallen with no hope of getting up? Have you been wounded and hurt by others? Are you so far down you think you'll never stand again? Don't despair. All Christians fall from time to time. Life knocks us off balance, making it hard – if not impossible – to get back on our feet. The cause of the fall is not as important as what we do while we're down. T.D. Jakes explains how – and Whom – to ask for help. In a struggle to regain your balance, this book is going to be your manual to recovery! Don't panic. This is just a test!

The God Factor
by James Giles

Is something missing in your life? Do you find yourself at the mercy of your circumstances? Is your self-esteem at an all-time low? Are your dreams only a faded memory? You could be missing the one element that could make the difference between success and failure, poverty and prosperity, and creativity and apathy. Knowing God supplies the creative genius you need to reach your potential and realize your dream. You'll be challenged as James Giles shows you how to tap into your God-given genius; take steps toward reaching your goal; pray big and get answers; eat right and stay healthy; prosper economically and personally; and leave a lasting legacy for your children.

Making the Most of Your Teenage Years
by David Burrows

Most teenagers live for today. Living only for today, however, can kill you. When teenagers have no plan for their future, they follow a plan that someone else devised. Unfortunately, this plan often leads them to drugs, sex, crime, jail, and an early death. How can you make the most of your teenage years? Discover who you really are – and how to plan for the three phases of your life. You can develop your skill, achieve your dreams, and still have fun.

The Biblical Principles of Success
Arthur L. Mackey Jr.

There are only three types of people in the world: 1) People who make things happen; 2) People who watch things happen; and 3) People who do not know what in the world is happening. *The Biblical Principles of Success* will help you become one who makes things happen. Success is not a matter of "doing it my way." It is turning from a personal, selfish philosophy to God's outreaching, sharing way of life. This powerful book teaches you how to tap into success principles that are guaranteed – *the Biblical principles of success!*

Flaming Sword
by Tai Ikomi

Scripture memorization and meditation bring tremendous spiritual power, however many Christians find it to be an uphill task. Committing Scriptures to memory will transform the mediocre Christian to a spiritual giant. This book will help you to become addicted to the powerful practice of Scripture memorization and help you obtain the victory that you desire in every area of your life. *Flaming Sword* is your pathway to spiritual growth and a more intimate relationship with God.

This is My Story
by Candi Staton

This is My Story is a touching autobiography about a gifted young child who rose from obscurity and poverty to stardom and wealth. With a music career that included selling millions of albums and topping the charts came a life of brokenness, loneliness, and despair. This book will make you cry and laugh as you witness one woman's search for success and love.

Another Look at Sex
by Charles Phillips

This book is undoubtedly a head turner and eye opener that will cause you to take another close look at sex. In this book, Charles Phillips openly addresses this seldom discussed subject and gives life-changing advice on sex to married couples and singles. If you have questions about sex, this is the book for you.

Four Laws of Productivity
by Dr. Mensa Otabil

Success has no favorites, but it does have associates. Success will come to anyone who will pay the price to receive its benefits. *Four Laws of Productivity* will give you the powerful keys that will help you achieve your life's goals. You will learn how to discover God's gift in you, develop your gift, perfect your gift, and utilize your gift to its maximum potential. The principles revealed in this timely book will radically change your life.

Single Life
by Earl D. Johnson

A book that candidly addresses the spiritual and physical dimensions of the single life is finally here. *Single Life* shows the reader how to make their singleness a celebration rather than a burden. This positive approach to singles uses enlightening examples from Apostle Paul, himself a single, to beautifully portray the dynamic aspects of the single life by serving the Lord more effectively. The book gives fresh insight on practical issues such as coping with sexual desires, loneliness, and preparation for your future mate. Written in a lively style, the author admonishes singles to seek first the kingdom of God and rest assured in God's promise to supply their needs... including a life partner!

Strategies for Saving the Next Generation
by Dave Burrows

This book will teach you how to start and effectively operate a vibrant youth ministry. This book is filled with practical tips and insight gained over a number of years working with young people from the street to the parks to the church. Dave Burrows offers the reader vital information that will produce results if carefully considered and adapted. It's excellent for pastors and youth pastors as well as youth workers and those involved with youth ministry.

The Call of God
by Jefferson Edwards

Since I have been called to preach, now what? Many sincere Christians are confused about their call to the ministry. Some are zealous and run ahead of their time and season of training and preparation while others are behind their time neglecting the gift of God within them. *The Call of God* gives practical instruction for pastors and leaders to refine and further develop their ministry and tips on how to nourish and develop others with God's call to effectively proclaim the gospel of Christ. *The Call of God* will help you to • Have clarity from God as to what ministry involves • Be able to identify and affirm the call in your life • See what stage you are in your call from God • Remove confusion in relation to the processing of a call or the making of the person • Understand the development of the anointing to fulfill your call.

Come, Let Us Pray
by Emmette Weir
Are you satisfied with your prayer life? Are you finding that your prayers are often dull, repetitive and lacking in spiritual power? Are you looking for ways to improve your relationship with God? Would you like to be able to pray more effectively? Then *Come, Let Us Pray* will help you in these areas and more. If you want to gain the maximum spiritual experience from your prayer life and enter into the very presence of God – *Come, Let Us Pray.*

Leadership in the New Testament Church
by Earl D. Johnson
Leadership in the New Testament Church offers practical and applicable insight into the role of leadership in the present day church. In this book, the author explains the qualities that leaders must have, explores the interpersonal relationships between the leader and his staff, the leaders' influence in the church and society and how to handle conflicts that arise among leaders.

Becoming A Leader
by Myles Munroe
Many consider leadership to be no more than staying ahead of the pack, but that is a far cry from what leadership is. Leadership is deploying others to become as good as or better than you are. Within each of us lies the potential to be an effective leader. *Becoming A Leader* uncovers the secrets of dynamic leadership that will show you how to be a

leader in your family, school, community, church and job. No matter where you are or what you do in life this book can help you to inevitably become a leader. Remember: it is never too late to become a leader. As in every tree there is a forest, so in every follower there is a leader.

Becoming A Leader Workbook
by Myles Munroe
Now you can activate your leadership potential through the *Becoming A Leader Workbook*. This workbook has been designed to take you step by step through the leadership principles taught in *Becoming A Leader*. As you participate in the work studies in this workbook you will see the true leader inside you develop and grow into maturity. ***"Knowledge with action produces results."***

Mobilizing Human Resources
by Richard Pinder
Pastor Pinder gives an in-depth look at how to organize, motivate, and deploy members of the Body of Christ in a manner that produces maximum effect for your ministry. This book will assist you in organizing and motivating your troops for effective and efficient ministry. It will also help the individual believer in recognizing their place in the body, using their God given abilities and talents to maximum effect.

The Minister's Topical Bible
by Derwin Stewart
The Minister's Topical Bible covers every aspect of the ministry providing quick and easy access to scriptures in a variety of ministry related topics. This handy reference tool can be effectively used in leadership training, counseling, teaching, sermon preparation, and personal study.

The Believer's Topical Bible
by Derwin Stewart
The Believer's Topical Bible covers every aspect of a Christian's relationship with God and man, providing biblical answers and solutions for all challenges. It is a quick, convenient, and thorough reference Bible that has been designed for use in personal devotions and group Bible studies. With over 3,800 verses systematically organized under

240 topics, it is the largest devotional-topical Bible available in the New International Version and the King James Version.

Available at your local bookstore or by contacting:

Pneuma Life Publishing
4451 Parliament Place
Lanham, MD 20706
(301) 577-4052

www.pneumalife.com

CPSIA information can be obtained
at www.ICGtesting.com
Printed in the USA
LVHW09s0834080918
589550LV00001BA/29/P